Penarth – the Story

Volume 1

By

Phil Carradice

Cover photograph by SCANAIR UK

ISBN No. 0954908600

Published by Penarth Press.
Printed by Beacon Printers Ltd, Penarth

Contents

Introduction

Penarth Head is the highest spot on the whole of the south Wales coast, soaring upwards for almost 200 feet and commanding all of the land and sea in the immediate vicinity. The headland is easily seen from many miles down the Bristol Channel, particularly with the spire of St Augustine's Church poised like an eastern minaret above the town. The headland and the church have always been something of a landmark for sailors and so it is appropriate that the story of Penarth is inextricably linked with the sea.

The origins of the name Penarth are a little unclear. It is quite possible that they derive from the Welsh words "pen" and "garth" which mean "head" and "ridge or headland" respectively. If this is so then the town is well named. Both the headland and the ridge on which the modern town now sits have played an important part in the development of Penarth.

Penarth Docks - the shipping industry made the town, gave it reason for existence.

Although the immediate area has a long and interesting history - and is, itself, more than deserving of special study - the town of Penarth is a relatively new phenomenon. Indeed, at less than two hundred years of age, Penarth would barely feature in any time chart of human existence. And yet, in that two hundred year period the town has been taken on a wild and extravagant roller coaster ride that has seen the heights of glorious success and the depths of dismal failure.

Brought into existence by the demands of industry, these days the town survives largely on the tourist trade. With its pier and Esplanade it remains caught in something of a time warp - even now, you feel, elegant Victorian ladies and gentlemen would not be out of place strolling along the promenade or taking tea in one of the many sea front cafes.

Yet the story of Penarth was not always quite so elegant as modern-day visitors might suppose. Once these streets were as dangerous as almost any Wild West frontier town. The history of this small community on the edge of the Bristol Channel is full of tales of enterprise and resolve, of luck and great judgement. It remains, quite simply, fascinating.

Penarth as most visitors would choose to remember it, full of happy and contented strollers walking along the Esplanade

I make no apology for what follows. This book is not a detailed, factual account of the town's development, stone by stone, year by year. It is, however, the story of Penarth, the story of how the place grew, how it developed, and also of some of the many individuals who helped with that development. The book tries to give an impression of what it was like to live in the town over the years, through good times and through bad. If it even partially succeeds in that aim then I shall be more than pleased.

Phil Carradice, 2004.

Penarth Pier, the jewel in the town's crown.

Horse drawn carriages wait at Penarth Pier c1908.

Chapter One: Early Days

Before the Town

For the first fifty years of the nineteenth century Penarth was little more than a tiny hamlet, the houses of poorly paid agricultural workers lying grouped around the flanks of Penarth Ridge. According to the 1801 census, as the nineteenth century began, Penarth's total population was just 71. Fifty years later that figure had increased to only 273.

In 1855, when plans were beginning to be laid for the creation of a new dock and community in the area, the combined population of Cogan, Llandough and Penarth - the three parishes that were to become the modern day town of Penarth - still barely reached four hundred. At this time all that existed were a scattering of cottages, the old St Augustine's Church (not the building that exists today) and an easterly facing pebble beach.

Penarth beach and headland are shown here in this nineteenth century print. It looks to be a wild and windswept place - notice that there is no pier, no promenade, no Esplanade.

The beach at Penarth had a flat, sandy strip below the high water mark but it was a spot rarely visited by people from the surrounding area. A few fresh water streams ran down the high, sloping cliffs making secluded dingles or dells in the woodland. The streams then ran across the beach and out into the Bristol Channel.

The beach at Penarth shortly after the Esplanade was created. Again, there is no pier but there is a bathing machine on the beach and the long slipway for the Yacht Club bisects the shingle.

The only building of any real note in the area was Kymin House. Kymin is probably a derivative of "ki", the old Celtic word for stream, and of "minni" which, in ancient Norse, meant "mouth of the stream." The connection with the Norse language is important. Viking settlements are known to have existed on nearby Flat Holm Island in the Bristol Channel and these streams, particularly the one that ran down the route of present day Beach Road, past the Kymin, would undoubtedly have been a major source of fresh water for the Norsemen.

Kymin House was built on the site of an earlier building, Kimmin Farm. Evidence exists of much earlier human occupation in the area, in fact from the Neolithic Period, a pair of axe heads having been discovered on the land around Erw'r Delyn School in the 1950s. Roman coins were also discovered when St Augustine's Church was being rebuilt in 1865 but speculation that Penarth Head was the site of a beacon station for the substantial Roman garrison at Cardiff remains exactly that - speculation.

The area around Penarth and Cardiff was raided, on a regular basis, by the Norsemen. They left records of their visitations in many of the local place names - holm, cog (from "kog", meaning marshland) and pill to name just three.

The Norman manor of Cosmeston was probably named after Robert de Constantin who held the lordship in the twelfth century. His base, Cosmeston Castle, has now long gone. It's exact location is uncertain but it probably lay somewhere in the vicinity of the reconstructed Cosmeston medieval village. Some scant remains were visible as late as 1940 but time and progress have now wiped this small fortification off the face of the earth. The old manor of Leckwith lay to the north of Llandough with the River Ely as its eastern boundary. Cogan, Llandough and Penarth itself made up the other ancient manors in the immediate vicinity of what was soon to become the town of Penarth.

The turbulent days of the Tudors and Stuarts, the Civil War and the Interregnum, left Penarth largely untouched but by the middle years of the nineteenth century revolutionary change was at hand. With the opening of Bute Dock in 1839 Cardiff had already become the main outlet for coal and iron that were now beginning to be mined in the valleys of south Wales. The mining and exporting of this Welsh coal began as a trickle and soon became a raging torrent. Before long the world-wide demand for Welsh anthracite had become insatiable.

The bay and Cardiff Docks are seen here from Penarth Head. The Penarth Hotel was later to become the J A Gibbs Home.

By 1854 the South Wales Coalfield was producing over 8,000,000 tons of coal each year and the docks at Cardiff were over stretched and close to saturation point. Something had to be done, and done quickly. The answer was found in the quiet backwater of the Ely River and in the tiny village of Penarth.

Penarth Docks - the Opening.

In 1855 a company under the chairmanship of Robert Clive of St Fagan's was formed with the aim of establishing a tidal harbour on the Ely River. The other main promoters of the company were Robert Clive's mother, Baroness Windsor, the coal magnate Crawshay Bailey, John Nixon and Lewis Davies. Most of the land around the proposed dock and harbour was owned by the Earls of Plymouth - the Windsor-Clive family, to give them their correct name. Lady Harriet Windor-Clive was a very wealthy woman. Her husband had died only the year before and on his death she became Baroness Windsor, effectively the owner of Penarth. In the months and years ahead her involvement was to be crucial for the new town.

The Coat of Arms of the Taff Vale Railway, the vibrant and efficient company that ran Penarth Dock.

Two Acts of Parliament in 1856 and 1857 granted permission for the Penarth Harbour and Railway Company to build docks at Penarth. The lower part of the Ely River was quickly converted into a tidal harbour and opened for trade while a rail link was laid to join up with the Taff Vale line at Cardiff. The Taff Vale was the railway company that brought most of the coal down the valleys to Cardiff and it was this vibrant, go-ahead organization that now took out a 999 year lease on the dock.

The tidal harbour was only the first part of an imaginative and far-sighted scheme - creation of a dock was the next stage. Work on the new dock began in 1859, the contractors being Messrs Smith and Knight. Progress was slow, however, and faulty work by the contractors resulted in an application to the Court of Chancery with the Directors being forced to take possession of the works themselves. They subsequently completed the construction under the direction of the engineers, Hawkshaw of London and Dobson of Cardiff.

The new dock was built on the north side of Penarth Head, using locally quaried stone, the jetties and pontoons fitting easily into a natural curve of the Ely River. Ten coal staithes were erected, each capable of handling 150 tons of "black gold" per hour. There were also a further two double staithes in the large Basin outside the dock and a number of steam driven cranes.

An early view of Penarth Dock, this shows the port dominated by sailing ships. Soon steam will replace sail but already the docks are a hive of industry.

The dock was officially opened on 10th June 1865. From early in the morning people flocked towards the docks to witness the opening ceremony. The ferryboat "Kate" brought hundreds of eager spectators across the bay from Cardiff while many more came by foot or by horse. Penarth headland was decorated with flags and bunting and dozens of small boats clogged the mouth of the river. A carnival or party atmosphere surrounded the proceedings, even though it was still very early in the morning. At 7.30am James Poole, Chairman of the Taff Vale Railway, climbed onto the podium and called for silence -

"Baroness Windsor," he declared, "was to have been present and assist in the ceremony of opening the dock, but by some unforeseen accident her ladyship has not arrived - - As time and tide wait for no man, I have been requested to open the dock in her name. I do so; and may God bless the undertaking. I now declare the Penarth Dock open."
("Cardiff and Merthyr Guardian", 16th June 1865)

The first ship to enter the new dock was the "William Cory," followed by the lifeboat "George Gay." Then came the "Lady Mary Windsor Clive" and, finally, the vessel belonging to the Seaman's Mission. Baroness Windsor arrived late and when the four ships had entered harbour she and Robert Clive together operated the lever to close the dock gates. The crowds of spectators and well-wishers then poured across the walkway to watch Baroness Windsor rename the lifeboat "Harriet."

After that it was simply a case of the invited guests (400 of them in all) making their way to the large marquee on the south side of the dock where a sumptuous breakfast awaited them. For the majority of the spectators, however, it was more a matter of sitting down in the sunshine wherever they could find a space and eating the frugal picnics they had brought with them to Penarth.

The Docks Grow.

Almost from the beginning the enterprise at Penarth was hugely successful. It was a tidal dock where, at high water, the gates would be left open to allow free movement of ships. So efficient was the system, and so skilled were the men who operated the cranes and coal staithes, that ships would enter the dock on one tide, fill their holds with coal and then leave for foreign shores on the very next tide.

In 1865 the amount of coal handled in the newly opened dock was an amazing 273,996 tons. In 1870 that figure was up to 900,000 tons and by 1882 it stood at two million tons per annum. From the start, however, the Directors of the Penarth Harbour and Dock Company realised that their facility was too small and, consequently, in 1880 they obtained permission to extend the dock to the westward. Four more coal staithes were to be added and the docks to be extended by 870 feet.

The giant coal staithes in the Basin dominate this shot, even though it seems to be a quiet time for the docks on the day the photograph was taken.

The new extension opened for business in 1884. From then on the docks regularly handled in excess of three million tons of coal a year with a peak of four and a half million being reached in 1913. Penarth Dock may have been small when compared to places like Cardiff and Barry but there was no denying its success and popularity with coal owners. A fast and efficient railway line connected the docks with almost every colliery in the Rhondda Fach and Rhondda Fawr, as well as places as far away as Aberdare and Merthyr. Even collieries in the Rhymney Valley sent coal to Penarth.

The first ship to use the pontoon at Penarth in 1909 was the "SS Ethelhilda." This view shows her being lifted onto the giant floating dock.

The first "Dock Master" at Penarth was the son of James Poole, Chairman of the Taff Vale Railway, the man who had actually opened the docks back in 1865. Whether the young Poole was happy with his sinecure or whether he worked hard at what must have been a demanding job is not known.

Repair facilities were soon added to the dock complex. A slipway was built in the harbour in 1879, just to the north of the dock itself. Here vessels of well over 200 feet could be beached and repaired. In 1909 a floating pontoon or dock was constructed for the company at Wallsend-on-Tyne and towed to Penarth. It arrived in October and was soon open for business. So large was the pontoon, however, that it had to be split into two before being brought inside the dock and then reassembled. This huge device, looking for all the world like a modern-day aircraft carrier, was capable of dry docking vessels up to 4500 tons.

Extension work is seen here being carried out on one of the dock buildings - almost from the start it was realised that the docks were too small and, within their first twenty years of existence, they had to be enlarged.

A small stretch of pebbles to the east of the Basin in front of the Custom House and Dock Buildings was known as Dock Beach. To the children of the area, who regularly swam and played here - happy, contented and a little incongruous in the lee of industry - it was invariably referred to as Donkey Beach. This strip of shingle and stone has now vanished forever under the infra-structure of the Cardiff Bay Barrage.

The Dock Buildings and Custom House were opened in 1865. The Dock Buildings had a wide range of shops on its ground floor, including a chemists, green grocers, butchers, ships chandlers and even a Post and Telegraphic Office. The site had once housed the Penarth Head Inn, frequented and maybe even owned by smugglers in the 1700s. The days of smuggling enterprises were largely over by this time, however, and the inn was demolished to make way for the new buildings. The wheel has, to some extent, come full circle as the place is now in use as a restaurant.

Communications.

Although Penarth and its dock lay close to Cardiff - at least as far as the crow flies - communication between the towns was never easy and for a long while the most effective way of travelling between the communities was actually by boat!

In 1878, however, the Penarth Extension Railway built a rail link from the station in the docks into the centre of Penarth town. This effectively created a passenger line between Penarth and Cardiff and communications immediately improved. Opened in

February 1878 the original Penarth Station had only one platform but traffic had soon become so heavy that a second platform was built and put into use in 1893. The station was now a grand affair, complete with iron footbridge linking Station Approach with nearby Plymouth Road. The almost obligatory "Railway Hotel" opened in the 1880s while, in the same decade, a beautiful and ornate Cabman's Shelter was erected in front of the station building.

The railway line to Cardiff ran down Cogan Bank, through the small Dingle Road Station and along a steep embankment between Cogan and Grangetown. The embankment made a highly effective barrier or dam to stop the water from the Ely River flowing into Cogan Pill.

A classic view of Penarth Dock station complete with iron footbridge.

This was the age of small railway companies, vibrant enterprises that had mushroomed up during the railway boom of the 1840s and '50s. Dozens, perhaps even hundreds, of these small lines existed in Britain, many of them running side by side with their competitors and serving the same purpose and similar communities. The two stations of Cogan and Penarth Dock Harbour are typical examples. They lay only a few hundred yards apart and a footpath even connected the two stations. Yet Cogan was part of the Barry Railway Company while Penarth Dock lay on the Taff Vale line. It was to be many years before the system was rationalized but in the meantime it gave passengers an incredible degree of flexibility in how and when they travelled.

This postcard view shows Penarth Town station and the octagonal cabman's shelter that once stood in front of it.

Penarth Town station was opened in 1878. This later view shows the station after a second platform had been built - the station's impressive iron footbridge can just be seen at the top left of the photograph.

The Penarth Dock and Harbour Station was renamed Penarth Dock Station in 1928. An interesting and unusual facility, it did not open on Sundays and, in the main, catered for rush hour trains. It closed in January 1962.

Penarth Dock and its station.

In 1867 Lord Bute built a road from Grangetown to Penarth, greatly easing the problem of road travel into Cardiff. Bute's new road crossed the Ely River by means of a bridge and, to aid His Lordship's coffers - and to pay for the expense of its creation - a toll was collected at this crossing point. Payment of the toll actually continued until 1952.

In the early days tolls were "a half penny for every ass, laden or un-laden - - - two shillings for every carriage drawn or impelled by steam or other power having more than two wheels." The language might have been quaint but the effect of the road on the community at Penarth was both liberating and quite startling.

Solomon Andrews, an early entrepreneur in the area, quickly negotiated charges through the toll for the buses and horse breaks he now began to run between Cardiff and Penarth. Andrews' "Three Horse Breaks" - three horses being needed because of the steepness of Cogan Hill - became famous and by 1895 he was running services from St Mary's Street at fifteen-minute intervals throughout the day. In 1902 there were over thirty vehicles employed on the route. A 5.20 am bus from Penarth even picked up passengers from their houses, at a cost of just one shilling, with a view to delivering them to the various Cardiff stations in time for their early morning trains.

Communication between Penarth Dock and Grangetown - and also to the harbour - was achieved by means of a chain ferry. This was opened, fare one penny, in June 1865 and was worked by two men operating a windlass on a floating platform or raft.

Soloman Andrews horse breaks ran from his offices at 112 Glebe Street into Cardiff. This shot shows one of the coaches ready to depart in the early years of the twentieth century.

The Cardiff and Penarth Steam Company had been founded in 1856, operating the steamer "Kate" out of Cardiff Docks. In 1882 she was joined by the "Iona" and "La Belle Marie." Between them they provided a twenty-minute shuttle service from the Pier Head in Cardiff to Penarth Docks. During the summer months the ferryboats also ran a service to the beach at Penarth where they landed passengers onto a set of moveable stages - not quite a pier and always difficult to negotiate for Victorian ladies in stays, bustles and crinolines.

Penarth Dock, full of ships taking on coal in 1908.

While the chain ferry had always been popular, particularly with workmen coming to the docks or Penarth from the Grangetown area, it was always subject to the vagaries of the weather and tide. Indeed, the ferry actually capsized on two occasions and was virtually unusable at low tide. In an effort to make the crossing easier and more practical work began on a subway under the river at the exact point where the old chain ferry used to cross. The subway opened in 1899, the toll for passage being one penny per pedestrian, two pence for a bicycle, three pence for a horse. Policemen and postmen were exempted from the toll. Tolls continued to be collected until 1941 and the subway closed, both entrances being sealed, on 30th September 1963.

The Docks - Decline and Closure.

Apart from a brief period at the end of the nineteenth century, Penarth Docks had always been highly productive. The low period in the 1890s can be attributed to sudden competition from newly opened Barry Docks, the brainchild of David Davies, Davies the Ocean as he is known, Wales' first millionaire. By the beginning of the First World War in 1914, however, things had stabilized and Penarth Docks were once more in a highly prosperous position.

The year 1922 brought the amalgamation of all the small railways across the country when these tiny organisations were suddenly grouped into four great companies. The Great Western Railway was probably thc only one of the "big four" to retain its distinctive identity, having already operated ovcr 3000 miles of track in both England and Wales prior to grouping.

The entrance to the dock was originally protected by the North and South Piers - they were later demolished when the marina was built. This view shows a cargo vessel at one of the piers.

The Taff Vale Railway, like all the other small lines, disappeared, swallowed up by the GWR. As well as track and railway routes the new company also inherited all the docks or ports that the small companies had previously run. And that, really, was the writing on the wall as far as Penarth was concerned.

With Cardiff and Barry Docks close at hand - both now controlled by the GWR - it was obvious that, should cuts need to be made, the smallest port would be the first to go. And the smallest port was Penarth.

The 1920s and '30s saw a drastic reduction in the amount of Welsh coal being exported as many lucrative markets dried up. The USA had captured the Canadian and South American trade while France and Italy, to whom so much Welsh coal had previously been sold, were now receiving huge amounts of German coal as part of the reparations decreed by the Treaty of Versailles. Added to all that the Royal Navy, which had always been a major user of Welsh steam coal, switched to oil for its capital ships. The result was depression, unemployment - and, ultimately, the closure of Penarth Docks.

Notice the wagons full of coal waiting to be loaded onto the ships in this later view of the dock. The port is already in decline, however, as the waterway is almost empty.

In fact Penarth held on quite doggedly for a long time. By 1936 the docks were still open but only just. The total trade figure, exports and imports, had dropped to just over 685,000 tons a year and on 6th July 1936 the docks finally closed for business. The last ship to leave the port, carrying a cargo of coal, was the "Amiens" which left for Europe on 4th July.

The Pontoon, Slipway and Ship Repairing Company in the harbour continued to battle on for some years, not finally closing down until 1963. Then the old pontoon was scrapped, partially sunk and converted into a municipal rubbish tip.

Horse breaks outside Albert Road Methodist Church at the beginning of the twentieth century. All seems well - the people do not know what is about to happen, either to their docks or the world in general.

With the outbreak of the Second World War Penarth Dock found a role for itself once again. The port was reopened and large tonnages of war material were dealt with on behalf of the Allied Governments. The north side of the dock was actually re-built in order to handle these war materials while four coal hoists on the southern side were made operational once more. In 1944 American forces established a repair base in the docks and over a hundred amphibious craft were dealt with in the port before hostilities ceased in 1945.

With the coming of peace and the subsequent reduction in traffic Penarth Dock was once again shut down. Some "moth balled" frigates and destroyers were laid up on the waterway for a number of years, as well as the paddle steamers of P and A Campbell. In 1963, however, the port finally closed for good.

Over the next twenty years the dock was filled in, the remaining buildings were demolished and the area landscaped. The 1980s and '90s saw a huge change to the environment as new housing and a state-of-the-art marina were built on the site.

There are still remains to be seen but, now, they are pitifully few - the last vestiges of the tidal harbour and the rotting remains of a few coal jetties. In general, though, the visitor to this part of Penarth would be hard pressed to realise that this site was once one of the most energetic and remarkable scenes of industry in the whole of south Wales.

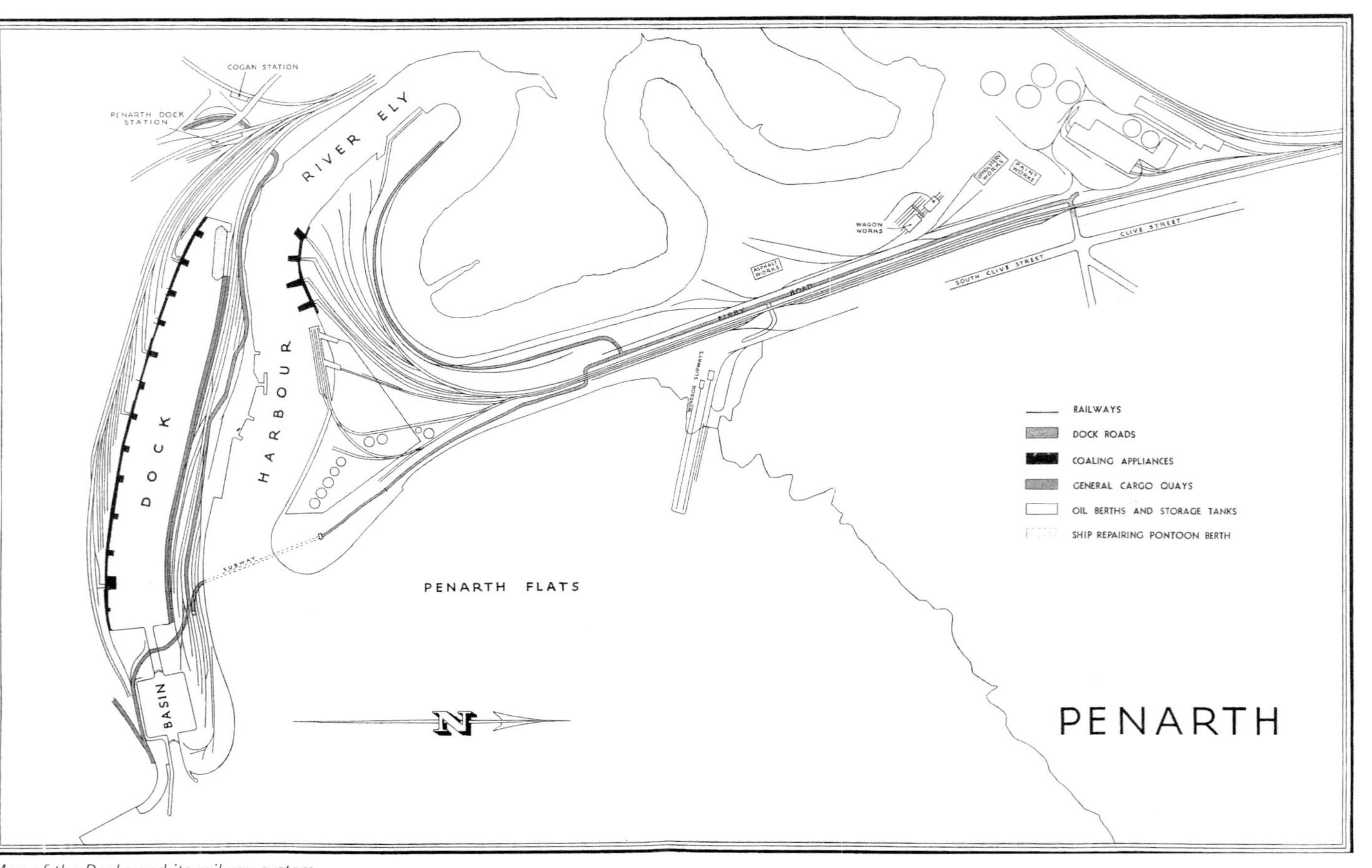

Map of the Docks and its railway system.

Chapter Two

The Town Grows

The town of Penarth grew rapidly in the wake of its new docks. In 1856 much of the land around the village or hamlet of Penarth was owned by Baroness Windsor and as workmen poured into the area to help build the docks complex it was soon clear that housing was desperately needed in order to accommodate them. With Baroness Windsor owning the land and having such a vested interest in the projected docks it was a simple matter to build cheap homes for the labourers who came from as far away as Ireland, Cornwall and Gloucester.

Ireland, in particular, seems to have provided a large number of the incomers. In the year 1863 alone 183 Irish workers arrived in the new town. Memories of the great famine of 1846-7 were still vivid and the dream of a fresh start in places like Penarth brought the Irish across St George's Channel in their boatloads.

Tradesmen quickly realised that a booming town like Penarth gave them limitless opportunities. This 1909 view shows Robert James ironmongers shop in the town.

Penarth did not just grow, it erupted like a volcano out of the land. In 1851 there had been no real streets or roads in the place, yet ten years later Ludlow Street, Salop Street and Glebe Street were all listed in official census returns. Indeed, the 1861 return gave the town a population of nearly 2000. In a brief ten year period the town's population had increased sevenfold. By 1871 that figure had risen again, this time to 2652.

In these early days Penarth was a wild and often dangerous place to live. Houses were usually occupied by two or more families - the 1861 census gives several examples of small terraced houses that held at least a dozen people. Many families soon learned that they could sub-let their rooms to lodgers in order to gain a little extra income.

Death was a common occurrence, either from accident or disease. With only limited public entertainment people resorted more and more to alcohol. Public houses proliferated, thirteen at least being in existence by 1861. There was thieving, pick pocketing and violence on a regular basis. As late as 1869 there was even evidence of smuggling going on in the town. Arguably it was almost an occupational hazard in any port and the "Cardiff Times" reported the incident in a very low key fashion under the headline "Smuggling Tobacco at Penarth." The paper commented that

"On Monday evening last, Mr Mitchell, Officer of Customs, detected John Fish and John Strutton, men belonging to the steamer 'Mary Nixon,' attempting to smuggle tobacco on shore."

Desertion from ship and prostitution were also rife. Fights, as drunken seamen and labourers fell out in public houses like "The Merrie Harrier," "The Golden Lion" and "The Clive Arms," were commonplace.

Like all British towns, cities and villages Penarth celebrated the coronation of George V in June 1911. This postcard shows the town's celebratory bonfire, built just to the south of St Augustine's Church.

Soon, however, a rather different type of person began to appear on the streets of Penarth. Well off businessmen from Cardiff, many of them being newly rich industrialists connected with the shipping trade, began to build houses for themselves in the town, well away from the stench and clutter of Cardiff. It made an interesting population mix. The houses of these wealthy individuals were elegant and substantial, particularly those in Marine Parade, and right from the beginning they saw themselves as being clearly different from the great mass of people in Penarth. With their arrival came civic pride, a desire to bring order to the town and the real beginnings of a truly structured Victorian society.

In November 1875 the three old parishes of Penarth, Cogan and Llandough were united and, six years later, the offices of the Penarth Local Board were opened in Albert Road. A Medical Officer was appointed, as well as an Inspector of Nuisances and an Inspector of Common Lodging Houses. The Windsor family handed over control of the main roads (and drainage) to the town, at no charge, and undoubtedly breathed a communal sigh of relief to see their creation finally looking after it's own affairs.

The town had been supplied with gas in 1854 while electricity was first generated by the Penarth Electric Company in 1898. With the establishing of a police station and fire brigade it seemed that all the trappings of local government were in place at last.

The ferryboat "Kate" is shown here, disembarking passengers onto the landing stage at Penarth beach. The popularity of the beach soon influenced Lord Windsor into developing the resort.

The Age Of Elegance.

It had always been intended - at least by the wealthy residents of the town - that Penarth, as well as being a centre for industry, should also become something of an elegant "watering hole," a place to rival Tenby in west Wales. The concept of a seaside break had gained in popularity during the nineteenth century and as Simon Adamson has said

"Hypochondria was a popular pastime in the upper echelons of British society - - - and an industry had grown up to cater for the wealthy sufferers of real or imaginary illness."
(Simon Adamson "Seaside Piers.")

Seawater - smelling it, bathing in it, even drinking it - was regarded as a potential cure for anyone with health troubles. Travelling to and from the seaside resorts was, initially, quite difficult but after 1815 journeys became much easier with the advent of steam passenger ships. When the railway system was laid across the country in the 1840s and 1850s the success of the seaside resort, as a concept, was assured. The wealthy upper echelons of Penarth society were determined that their town would not miss out.

By the early 1880s this section of the town's population, and the aspiring middle classes below them, were already making complaints about "the rabble from the hills," people who were monopolizing the beach at Penarth. They were referring to visitors or trippers from Cardiff and the valleys beyond, people who, in the summer months, came on the ferryboats run by the Cardiff Steam Navigation Company to spend the day on Penarth beach.

Dozens of holiday makers enjoy the sun and sea in this view of the beach below Penarth Head. Notice the searchlight towers on the right of the photograph and the sheer walkway that took soldiers up to the top of the cliffs.

According to several newspaper reports at the time many of these "unwanted visitors" actually had the temerity to dry their bathing dresses on lines or wires they had slung along the beach. Some of them even bathed naked in the sea! It was not quite open warfare between the day trippers and the upper class residents of Penarth but a number of prosecutions soon occurred, the idea being that everyone should know his or her place in the fragile fabric of society - if it needed the strong arm of the law to keep people where they belonged then that was what would be provided. Not for nothing did the Victorian gentry at their divine worship sing

"The rich man in his castle,
The poor man at his gate,
God made them high and lowly
And ordered their estate."

In the main, however, unwelcome visitors were not to be persecuted or even prosecuted but were simply to be discouraged from visiting an area that was clearly not for "their sort." Consequently, in a distinct attempt to upgrade the resort the Windsor family - still major landowners in the area - conceived a plan that would exclude the rougher elements of the tourist trade and make Penarth a resort to rival not only Tenby but also English destinations like Brighton and Worthing. It was a deliberate ploy, meaning that, unlike the fashionable towns on the south coast of England, Penarth did not expand from an upper class resort to take in working people. Rather, it was the other way round.

Robert Forrest, Lord Windsor's estate manager at St Fagan's, was instrumental in getting things going. Under his direction, Windsor Gardens, an elegant park on the hill above the beach, was duly laid out and opened in 1880. A fee of one penny was charged for admission -that in itself was enough to discourage some people!

In 1885 the town swimming baths were opened. Set in an attractive and elegant building, capped by a cupola and the effigy of a leaping dolphin, the baths were located on the sea front and cost over £7000 to build. These costs were born by Lord Windsor and by the Local Board. Initially the baths were fed by salt water from two reservoirs in nearby Alexandra Gardens, the water being pumped up from the Bristol Channel at high water. Only later did the baths turn to fresh water. There were actually two pools in the complex, as well as several other amenities that now, with hindsight, offer a clear indication of what Robert Forrest and Lord Windsor had in mind for the town.

The larger of the two pools was 79 feet long, the smaller one just 52 feet. Hot and cold slipper baths were available and the larger of the pools could be boarded over and used as a gymnasium. Sometimes roller-skating also took place when the boarding was down.

The Esplanade Hotel was built and opened in 1887 alongside the baths. Constructed from locally produced bricks and imported Bath stone, the hotel was an elegant and artistically pleasing creation with superb views across the Bristol Channel.

A few hundred yards away, along the seafront, lay the town's Yacht Club. Built in several distinct stages and opened in 1880, a long slipway for the yachts extended down the beach in front of the clubhouse. Even in the early days of the town, it seemed, boating on the Channel was extremely popular.

Penarth Yacht Club was founded in 1880, the building being the height of Victorian elegance.

The town baths and the Esplanade Hotel were an important part of the plan to "upgrade" Penarth. Elegant and attractive, the two buildings dominated the sea front.

Forrest's supreme achievement, however, was the creation of the Esplanade, the road and walkway along the sea front. Between 1883 and 1884, he worked in conjunction with Henry Snell, architect for the Windsor estate, and a consultant by the name of Barry. Together they created Forrest's vision for the Esplanade, a long and elegant carriage road connecting Marine Parade and Plymouth Road that effectively made a circular drive around the town of Penarth.

Thirty-six feet wide, the road ran along the sea front in a north-south direction, providing an inviting promenade for strollers. At its southern end the road climbed sharply up Cliff Hill, over 40,000 cubic yards of rubble having been cut from the hillside in order to make Forrest's dream complete.

Penarth as Lord Windsor and his agent Robert Forrest envisaged it - refined, quiet, just the place for a leisurely stroll by the sea.

The effect was startling. No longer did visitors and locals have to pick their way across the stony beach. Now they had a modern, flat surface that would not damage clothes or shoes. All that was now lacking was a promenade pier.

Penarth Pier

The curious British love affair with seaside piers has its origins in the early methods of transporting holiday makers to the coastal resorts - by boat. Huge difficulties were encountered in actually landing passengers. Many had to be ferried ashore in gigs or rowing boats and that invariably resulted in heavy dresses and topcoats becoming saturated by seawater. At Ryde on the Isle of Wight day-trippers were even given piggybacks through the waves on the shoulders of brawny porters. It was not the answer, of course - that came in the shape of the famous seaside pier.

Day trippers sit on the beach and enjoy the sun - no bathing costumes here, you will notice!

Britain's first real pier at Ryde opened in 1814 while Brighton's Chain Pier was built between 1822 and 1823. Over the next few years dozens of seaside piers followed, right around the shore of Britain.

It quickly became apparent that people were using piers for reasons other than embarking or disembarking from ferries. From the 1840s onwards the word "promenade" began to feature in the advertisements of pier companies. Casual strollers, it seemed, people who were willing to pay their penny to walk along the decking, were becoming an important source of income for the pier companies.

When the 1871 Bank Holiday Act gave workers (not all but some, certainly) the right to statutory holidays or short breaks from work, there was an outbreak of pier building. No self respecting seaside resort could be without its long stretch of iron and wooden decking where ladies and gentlemen could stroll or sit in deckchairs, contemplating the sun, sand and sea air. They could have been at sea, albeit without the discomfort of seasickness.

On 29th December 1888 "The Western Mail" published an article, stating

"The prospectus for the Penarth Promenade and Landing Pier Company Ltd, has just been issued - - - Lord Windsor, the owner of the foreshore, has granted the necessary licence for 99 years at the nominal rent of £25 per annum. It is expected that the pier will supply a long-felt want not only to the inhabitants of Penarth - - - but to the inhabitants of the surrounding district."

The Company, of which many local businessmen were Directors, had to raise the necessary money and shares at £5 each were a heavy expenditure. There was, therefore, a delay before construction began. In the autumn of 1893 a rumour began to spread, stating that the Company proposed to buy a second hand pier from the town of Douglas on the Isle of Man. Immediately there was an outcry in Penarth. The Douglas Pier had already endured 25 years of battering from the elements and the people of Penarth wanted a new pier of their own, not somebody else's cast off. In the end Douglas Pier went to Rhos-on-Sea and work began on the brand new Penarth Pier in April 1894.

The Pier Is Opened

Penarth Pier was built by the Manchester engineers James and Arthur Mayoh. They may not have had quite the same pedigree as the designer Eugenius Birch, the doyen of pier builders, but they were well known in their field, had already built piers at Morecambe and Great Yarmouth, and later went on to build one at the Mumbles outside Swansea.

Once work began the new pier quickly took shape. The huge iron legs were cast in nearby foundries and then brought out to the shore on flat-bedded trailers. They were then inserted into bore-holes that had been dug on the sea bed. The decking and railings were laid on top. The winter of 1894-5 was a cold one but the workmen ploughed on with their task and by February 1895 everything was finally ready.

Measuring 658 feet long and 25 feet wide the pier had a landing stage at its seaward end and ornate iron railings around the wooden decking. Two shops, each with pointed, lead covered roofs, stood each side of the entrance and there were also a pair of elegant public shelters half way down the pier.

Opening day was set for 13th April 1895 and despite cold, wet weather a large crowd gathered to witness the event. The pier was decorated with bunting and the Cogan Brass Band played a selection of tunes for the entertainment of the crowd. The two paddle steamers "Bonnie Doon" and "Waverley" approached the landing stage, a salute was fired from the pier and amid cheers and laughter Mr H F Edwards, the engineer and designer, was the first person to step ashore. There were no speeches and the two paddlers simply discharged and took on passengers before setting sail for Weston-Super-Mare. The pier was open for business.

Penarth - Seaside Resort

With its new promenade pier up and running Penarth was soon attracting visitors by the hundreds. Many of them came on the paddle steamers that now regularly used the pier as a landing stage.

Pleasure steamers had operated in the Bristol Channel for several years before the pier opened. The first excursion steamer on the waterway had been the "Bonnie Doon." She had been brought to the area by a consortium of Bristol businessmen in 1886. From 1888, however, Captain Alex Campbell and his brother Peter moved their paddler "Waverley" from the Clyde and began a series of cruises that eventually eclipsed all competition and made the name of their White Funnel paddle steamers synonymous with cruising on the Channel.

Cruising on the Bristol Channel was a popular pastime. This photograph shows the "Bonnie Doon", one of the first paddle steamers to call at Penarth.

In the early days, however, there was plenty of competition from firms like Edwards-Robertson of Cardiff, the Lady Margaret Steamship Company and the Barry Railway Company. It was a wild, exciting time and complaints about the pleasure steamers were common.

On Saturday 2nd May 1896 the boat keeper of Penarth Yacht Club was thrown out of his boat by the wash from the paddler "Cambria." A few days later the cutter "Halogan" was actually sunk by a steamer. Not long afterwards the "Lady Margaret", with Alex Campbell himself on the bridge, swamped a rowing boat while approaching the pier at high speed. Seven people were thrown into the water and the Inspector of Boats had to dive in to save them.

Part of the problem undoubtedly lay with the paddle steamers as the first ship to reach the landing stage invariably picked up the waiting trippers. Therefore speed was everything. At the same time, there were dozens of small boats operating off Penarth beach. They were like flies around a honey pot and when filled to the gunwales with passengers - most of them in heavy, restrictive clothing - would have been unwieldy at the best of times.

Once Penarth Pier was up and running people quickly realised that for just a few shillings they could enjoy steamer trips along the Welsh and English coasts - the success of the pier was guaranteed.

There were a number of suicides off the pier in these early days. On 30th April 1901 Margaret Davies threw herself off the seaward end, the "Penarth Observer" commenting that

"It is to be hoped a careful watch will be kept upon this spot for some time, lest her success - if it may so be called - should lead to a crop of imitators."

Penarth Pier is shown here in 1904 - notice the two elegant shelters, one each side of the pier, half way down its length.

Entertainment!

Promenading up and down the pier was probably the main entertainment in these early years. People visited in their thousands while the pleasure steamers kept calling in a continuous stream, full to bursting with eager holiday makers. Overcrowding on the paddlers was a continual problem, as the pleasure cruising companies fought for supremacy in the Channel. On 11th July 1900 Captain Ashford of the "Glen Rosa" was found guilty of carrying 797 passengers when his vessel was licensed for only 541. At the same time Captain M'Cloud of the "Scotia" was charged with overloading his ship by an amazing 357 extra bodies! Health and safety, indeed!

In 1907 a wooden pavilion was built at the seaward end of the pier. The people of Penarth had long been calling for such a facility but the Directors of the Pier Company had been reluctant to risk the financial commitment until they had achieved an adequate return on their original investment. The success of the pier, however, more or less forced the Company's hand. If Penarth did not have a pavilion for entertainment then the holiday makers would simply go elsewhere.

Known as the Penarth Pier Bijou Pavilion, the new hall was first managed by Oscar Mills and over the next few years offered a wide selection of acts and entertainment to keep visitors happy. Admission prices to the pavilion ranged from one shilling down to three pence and on Sunday evenings - an unusual occurrence in these times of strict religious observation - military band and orchestral concerts were offered to the populace.

Little Marjorie Fountain, the soloist of Lila Fields English Dancers - just one of many acts that appeared on Penarth Pier.

In 1910 Oscar Mills presented his Royal Court Entertainers at 3.15 each afternoon throughout the season. They then re-appeared at 7.30 in the evening. Mills relinquished his lease on the Bijou Pavilion at the end of 1910, his place being taken by Alfred Newton who was to run the pier entertainments for the next twenty years.

Newton brought in new acts such as The Court Jesters and The Mad Hatters. He also offered the occasional farce or light play. He engaged "up market" entertainers such as Lila Fields' Celebrated Company of English Girls, featuring a Russian ballet with Little Marjorie Fountain as the solo ballerina.

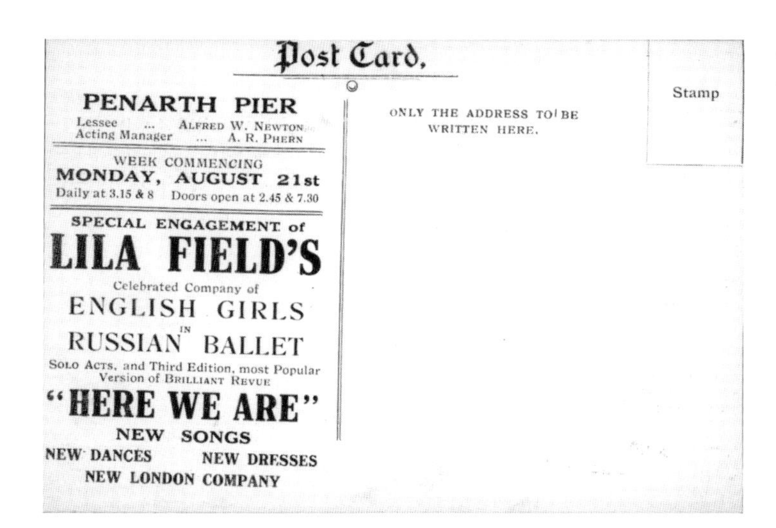

Post Card.

PENARTH PIER
Lessee ... ALFRED W. NEWTON
Acting Manager ... A. R. PHERN

WEEK COMMENCING
MONDAY, AUGUST 21st
Daily at 3.15 & 8 Doors open at 2.45 & 7.30

SPECIAL ENGAGEMENT of
LILA FIELD'S
Celebrated Company of
ENGLISH GIRLS
IN
RUSSIAN BALLET
SOLO ACTS, and Third Edition, most Popular
Version of BRILLIANT REVUE
"HERE WE ARE"
NEW SONGS
NEW DANCES NEW DRESSES
NEW LONDON COMPANY

ONLY THE ADDRESS TO BE
WRITTEN HERE.

Stamp

An advertising postcard giving advance notice of the "Special engagement" of Lila Fields Dancers.

By the summer of 1914 Penarth Pier boasted shops and tea rooms, Salter's Pier Café and Tea Gardens being particularly popular. There were more refreshment rooms in the Esplanade Hotel and on the ground floor of the flats that had been built on the Esplanade in 1904. Later, on the north end of the beach, in the area known as the Dardanelles, were dozens of tented refreshment stalls. These included the famous Mrs Norman's Cockle Stall.

This unusual shot of Penarth and the pier was taken from the air in the early days of aerial photography.

A classic view of the pier entrance, showing Salter's Pier Café and, on the banner over the entrance, advertising "Montague's Mountebanks," that week's special entertainment.

Penarth at War

The sudden outbreak of war in August 1914 brought the times of ease and plenty to an abrupt end. Almost immediately several of the Bristol Channel paddle steamers were requisitioned by the Admiralty for conversion into minesweepers. Many of the pier personnel also joined up, Piermaster Leonard serving for four years and being torpedoed while serving on board the battleship "Majestic" during the Dardanelles campaign.

Some time during the early war years - the exact date is a little unclear - Penarth Pier was requisitioned by the army. It was garrisoned by a detachment of Royal Engineers and a searchlight positioned on its seaward end. Two field guns were stationed on Penarth Head, the idea being that they would work in conjunction with the searchlight should Cardiff be attacked by German surface raiders.

Soldiers were billeted in the shops along the Esplanade or housed in tents on the rough ground between the Beach Shelter and the Yacht Club. The commander of the detachment, Lieutenant Christopher John Evans, had his office in a hut alongside the Bijou Pavilion. The unit also had a mascot, a black and white terrier known as Tiger. The dog was often to be seen racing up and down the pier, totally ignoring the drop below. His daredevil antics were, eventually, his undoing as Tiger later fell from the cliffs after one of his bursts of energy and was killed instantly.

In 1917 the Royal Engineers moved off the pier onto Penarth Head. Their searchlights were re-positioned on specially constructed towers at the foot of the cliff. These structures remained in place for many years, a reminder of the part played by the town in the Great War. An almost vertical set of steps linked the platforms with the top of the cliff - not the place to tarry on a dark, windy night. The searchlight platforms survived two wars only to be destroyed by a cliff fall in the 1960s.

This wonderful postcard shows one of the White Funnel paddlers at the end of the pier, loaded to the gunwales with eager trippers. It also gives a good impression of the Bijou Pavilion that stood on the pier for over twenty years.

There was some limited use of the pier by the general public during the war years and the Royal Engineers even put on one or two shows for the locals, using the Bijou Pavilion as their base. Inevitably, however, the pier took a battering during this period and at the end of hostilities the Pier Company put together a claim for £7228 in compensation. The Company stated that much of the damage had been caused by the heavy boots of the soldiers as they paraded up and down the decking. Army orders were explicit on this point - soldiers had to wear plimsoles whilst walking on the pier, not boots. The Pier Company was offered only £353 in compensation.

It was a cruel blow for the Directors and for the town. "The Penarth News" for 7th December 1922 declared that

"Nobody can justify the absurd award of the War Compensation Court of £353 - - - it is an ill reward for war service and wretchedly unjust to the people who have to bear the financial burden."

That was one of the more sober judgements. "The Penarth Observer" was far more explicit in its views -

"Without doubt more would have been paid for commandeering a fried fish shop in a back street."

The issue was raised in Parliament but Stanley Baldwin, then Chancellor of the Exchequer, replied that he did not propose "to suggest to the Tribunal that a re-hearing of the case should take place."

Fulminate and complain as much as they might, the local papers, like the local people and the Pier Company, were faced by the stark realities of the situation. The army had finished with the pier; all appeals had failed; from now on Penarth and its pier were on their own.

When war came in 1914 many of the paddle steamers were called up for duty. This shows the "Glen Avon," in war colours.

Penarth did not enjoy the war years. By and large the beaches were empty and, with the pier commandeered for war service, there seemed little to smile about. When the pier was given back in 1919 its dilapidated condition almost brought the town to its knees.

A busy day on the beach at Penarth.

Chapter Three

Taking Shape

Windsor Road in the 1930s. By this time it was the main street of the town, full of shops and local businesses, but originally it had only three buildings in its entire length.

The town of Penarth had begun to assume the general shape that we see today in the years immediately after 1856. The main shopping area in these early days was Glebe Street, the road having been carved out of (and named after) the original glebe or church land given to St Augustine's Priory back in the twelfth century. The Priory was based in Bristol and not only did it own most of the land in the area, it also built the original St Augustine's Church. Much of the Priory land was sold off after the Dissolution of the Monasteries during the reign of Henry V111. What little land the church retained had been bought by the Windsor/Plymouth family in 1853.

Development of the town was rapid and by 1871 there were 98 properties in Glebe Street alone. By contrast Windsor Road, now the town's main thoroughfare, had only eighteen. A few years earlier there had been just three - the police station, "The Windsor Hotel" and the "St Fagan's Castle Inn." Originally, there were no buildings at all on the south side of the road, just fields stretching away into the distance. Houses with front gardens were built on the north side of the road but, as the town developed, these were replaced by shops and the gardens were removed. This allowed for the wide pavement frontage that still exists today.

The butcher's shop belonging to R H Lea - what would Health and Hygiene say today about the meat and carcasses?

An advertising card for Lea's Butchers, almost a work of art.

The Cornerswell shopping area did not develop until the 1920s but Stanwell Road (originally known as Parish Road) had been in existence for many years. Turner House was built in 1888 to house James Pyke Thompson's collection of Turner paintings and was soon opened to the public. It is now part of the National Museum of Wales.

Turner House Gallery, built originally to house the paintings of none other than Turner.

The Stanwell Road shopping area of Penarth - just look at the sheer elegance of the buildings.

This rare postcard shows the Windsor Arcade c1905. Looking at it now it seems that very little has changed in the Arcade over a hundred years. Shopping arcades were once a feature of all British cities and towns. Most of them have now dissapeared, thanks to modern developments, but Cardiff remains the premier example of a town full of beautiful old victorian arcades.
Penarth's Windsor Arcade is the only example in the seaside town. It is full of atmosphere, allowing visitors a brief impression of what shopping would have been like in the early years of the Twentieth Century.

Charabanc outings were always popular, even in places like Penarth - which was where most people came on their outings. So where are they going? Incidentally, the building behind the charabanc was the old Fire Station for the town.

Dingle Halt, shown here in the 1950s when it actually had two platforms.

Church and Chapel

Five Anglican churches - Llandough, Leckwith, Cogan, Penarth and Lavernock - existed in the area at the beginning of the nineteenth century. Of these, the famous St Augustine's on Penarth Head, always a landmark for sailors beating up the Channel, had been a site of religious significance for over 800 years.

The old church of St Augustine's - Top Church as it was known in the town - had a low squat tower and was demolished in 1865. A larger church was needed in the rapidly expanding town and Baroness Windsor donated £10,000 for the building work. William Butterfield, the renowned designer of Keble College in Oxford, was employed as architect and Baroness Windsor laid the foundation stone on 8th June 1865. The first service was held in the church on 11th September 1866.

The new building did not attract universal approval. Many people thought it was too beautiful and artistic for a place of worship. The essential purpose of a church, they said, was to worship God, not gaze at the construction itself!

St Augustine's Church was always known as Top Church in Penarth. Standing on the crest of Penarth Ridge it is easy to see why. This is the new church built in 1865 - a religious building of one sort or another has stood here for 800 years.

The Rev J Thomas, Rector at St Augustine's from 1901 until December 1910, just one of the many preachers and pastors who have administered to their flocks in the town.

All Saints Church was originally built of iron and stood on the corner of Rectory and Stanwell Roads, opposite the present day library. The church was relocated to Victoria Square in 1890, the building being designed by John Coates Carter. It was damaged by a serious fire in 1927 and then, in 1941, was almost destroyed in an air raid during the Second World War. Services were held in the Parish Hall until the building could be put back into order. It finally reopened in 1954.

The influx of Irish labourers - to build Penarth Docks, to work in the mines and iron foundries of south Wales or simply to escape the grinding poverty of their native country - meant that there was soon a dire need for a Catholic church. In 1864, for example, Father

Nedeloc gave an open air mass for a huge gathering of 600 workmen who were involved in constructing the docks. In 1876 land was bought at the top of Arcot Street and a church and school built. The present day St Joseph's Church in Wordsworth Avenue was built as a replacement in 1914.

Non-conformists were also well catered for. The first recorded involvement of Baptists in the town came in 1858 when an unknown lay-preacher held a service in a cottage in Glebe Street. Tabernacle Chapel was built between 1870 and 1871, the foundation stone being laid by Cardiff industrialist Richard Cory. The original building cost only £1000 but it was rebuilt and extended in 1894 at the cost of a further £3000.

John Wesley never preached in Penarth but he was active in the immediate vicinity, working in Dinas Powis and the Vale of Glamorgan. His brother Charles wrote "Jesu, lover of my soul" - later put to music as "Aberystwyth" by Penarth resident Joseph Parry.

Parry was an active member and church organist at Christchurch in Stanwell Road. Born at Merthyr Tydfil, he lived in Penarth for several years before his untimely death in 1903. The church itself was built in 1897 and offered to the Congregationalists by Solomon Andrews in exchange for the site of their original church on the corner of Windsor Road. The beautiful Gothic style church with its 100 foot high spire was, unfortunately, demolished in the late 1980s.

Christchurch has now been demolished but it stood for many years, dominating the centre of town with its 100 foot spire. Joseph Parry used to play the organ in the church.

Trinity Methodist Church was founded in 1891, the church rooms being set well back from Stanwell Road because the Methodists wanted to preserve a tree in their grounds. A new building was opened on 2nd January 1901 and the original iron church was sold and rebuilt in Barry. The church has a long and fascinating history, not least being the fact that one of its Sunday School teachers drowned when the "Titanic" sank in 1912 - a plaque in the church commemorates the place where he used to teach.

Albert Road Church stands on the other side of town and was opened in 1906 after a fire had destroyed the Methodist Church in Arcot Street. The site of the old Arcot Street Church was later acquired by the Anglicans, soon opening up as St Paul's.

Albert Road Methodist Church, built in 1906.

The Salvation Army had established a presence in Penarth as early as 1884, basing themselves in many different homes over the years. In October 1922 their premises over a garage in Salop Street were destroyed by fire, all of the band's instruments perishing in the flames. Only the Salvation Army flag was saved, having been kept at the home of Colour Sergeant Wallace - Tommy Dodd as he was always known in the town. After the fire the officers of Tabernacle Chapel kindly loaned their premises to the Salvationists until such time as they could obtain a new home.

The Salvation Army Band, complete with big bass drum, pose happily for the photographer in one of the town's side streets - they certainly couldn't do that today!

Schools

Formal schooling, available for every child in Britain, did not exist until 1870 when Forster's Education Act was passed by Parliament. Prior to that most education was voluntary. In practice what tended to happen was education at the extremes. The children of the wealthy classes were educated because their parents could afford to pay for it, usually in one of the great public schools like Eton or Harrow. The children of the very poor - and often very delinquent - were also quite well catered for, in quantity if not in quality, by the workhouse schools and reformatories. For the vast majority, those occupying the middle ground, almost nothing was available.

The church tried to fill the gap, Anglican and Non-conformist bodies alike. The National Society, with its roots in the established church, began life in 1811 while the British and Foreign School Society was founded by Quaker Joseph Lancaster three years later. Based on the well-known Monitorial System where bright children were used to instruct the rest of the class, these two societies offered the main educational input in the early years of Queen Victoria's reign.

A National School was opened in Penarth in 1863, standing on the corner of High Street and Plassey Street. The cost of setting up the school was borne by Baroness Windsor - another example of the incredible philanthropy shown by the family towards the town they had created - and the first formal educational establishment in Penarth opened its doors to 175 eager children.

This 1899 view shows a class of girls at Albert Road Board School. They appear to be taking part in a sewing lesson - equipping them for the role they will play in life.

The County School - previously the Intermediate School, soon to be the town Grammar School and, ultimately, one of the top comprehensives in Wales.

Forster's Education Act effectively created School Boards to build new schools wherever there was a need. The Penarth School Board came into existence in 1874 and their Board School was duly opened in Albert Road on 18th September 1876. Interestingly, the school buildings were designed by the same Henry Harris who co-designed the swimming baths on the Esplanade.

Secondary education in Britain came in the years after 1888 when the newly formed County Councils were made responsible for the provision of both elementary and secondary education. The Welsh Intermediate Education Act was passed a year later, making it a legal obligation to provide secondary education for all young people, a dozen years before similar legislation was passed in England.

Work on the Penarth Intermediate and Technical School commenced in 1894, Lord Windsor donating a large tract of land for the purpose. The school was situated in Archer Road, catering for 200 boys and girls, and opened in January 1897. It was to be another fifty years before Butler's Act of 1944 created the Tripartite System, a network of grammar, secondary modern and technical schools. As a consequence of this Act the old Intermediate School was re-designated as Penarth Grammar School while Penarth Secondary Modern School was built and opened in 1958. When comprehensive education replaced the Tripartite System the two schools became known as Stanwell and St Cyres respectively.

Westbourne House School, one of many private schools and colleges that were founded in Penarth.

Penarth has a long and distinguished record of offering first class "special" education. The Penarth Hotel in Paget Place was opened by the Taff Vale Railway Company in 1868. Never a great commercial success, by the closing years of World War One the hotel was empty and forlorn. When, in April 1917, Major John Angel Gibbs of the Cardiff shipping family was killed leading his troops on the Menin Road in France, his widow purchased the building and donated it to the National Children's Homes and Orphanage - on the condition that it was run as a Nautical Training School. The new establishment was designated the J A Gibbs Home and was opened in November 1918.

The Gibbs Home had strong links with nearby Albert Road School. Pupils would attend there in the day, then begin nautical studies at night and continue them once they had reached statutory school leaving age. Nautical training took place in the old stable block alongside the main building. Here lay HMS "Mal de Mer" - a platform on rollers that could be pulled or pushed to simulate the motion of a ship at sea. It supposedly taught boys to cope with sea-sickness whilst trying to keep their minds (and stomachs) on the important task of holding a ship on course. Quite how successful the device was remains unclear!

HMS "Mal de Mer," the sea sickness machine at the J A Gibbs Home. Here boys were trained for careers at sea and the sea sickness machine was intended to get them used to the motion of a ship - as well, of course, as teaching them how to steer.

At one time there were nearly a hundred boys living and training at the Gibbs Home, the place being run largely by a small group of Methodist Sisters. The placement of one boy, Edwin Meek, was funded by the Titanic Relief Fund as his mother had been drowned in the 1912 disaster. Another pupil, Roland Wixey, was killed in 1931 when he fell over the cliff at the top of the grounds. Attempting to recover a handkerchief that had lodged part-way down the cliff, Wixey fell one hundred and fifty feet and died as a result of his injuries.

Although ostensibly a Nautical Training School, not all the Gibbs Home boys went to sea. Over seventy were sent to begin new lives in Canada, part of the now infamous child emigration scheme run by Dr Barnardo and other child-care specialists in the nineteenth century. Unlike many other charities, NCH was able to monitor its placements in Canada through the use of its Hamilton branch. While some of the Gibbs Home boys undoubtedly endured hard times in their new country, most of them were able to settle down and thanks to the monitoring system were able to build themselves successful lives.

In 1936 the Gibbs Home changed its role and function, becoming an Approved School for delinquent boys. At this time it was unique in being the only Approved School to send its pupils to outside school (Albert Road). This came to an end after World War Two when a purpose-built educational block was erected on site. The Home duly changed its name to Headlands School and now runs as a special school for EBD boys and girls.

Boys at the Gibbs Home line the mast at the top of the school grounds. From here it was a sheer 150 foot drop onto the beach or, if you were lucky and the tide was in, into the Bristol Channel.

Penarth was also the site of Wales' first purpose-built school for children with physical disabilities. Ysgol Erw'r Delyn was opened in 1972, quickly gaining a name for itself under the charismatic leadership of head teacher John Garrett. Ashgrove School for the Deaf was opened the same year.

Due to the rapid growth of the town's population over the years Penarth has been forced to regularly create new schools. The first of these was Victoria Primary which opened its doors in Cornerswell Road in 1897. Other new schools included Fairfield (1954), Evenlode (1969), Llandough (1970) and a new Catholic school in Sully Road in 1970.

A number of small private schools also made Penarth their home at one time or another. These have included places like Westwood College, located in the present Conservative Club building, Westbourne House School and St Maeburn's Ladies College which opened in Marine Parade in 1886. There have been many other small educational establishments - private schools, nurseries and so on, far too many to mention here. Suffice to say that they have all continued the town's noble tradition of offering quality education for all elements of society.

Pubs and Inns

Like any port or harbour town Penarth has always had a wide selection of public houses and inns to cater for the sailors from visiting ships. However, as a notable seaside resort it has also had to provide rather more salubrious hostelries, places where day trippers and holiday makers could pause for a moment and watch the world go by.

The development of the town coincided with a significant change of life in Britain. Ready money, in the form of a weekly wage, was beginning to replace more traditional, agrarian styles of existence like barter and subsistence farming. As the century went on many people actually had money in their pockets - spare money - for the first time in their lives. And they were not afraid to spend it. For some people alcohol seemed like a good place to start.

"The Ship Hotel" was one of Penarth's earliest public houses. Built in the 1850s, it stood in a prime position on the corner of Glebe Street and Maughan Street. It's reputation, however, was not good.

In 1869 Inspector Adams of the Penarth Police was called to deal with an affray outside the hotel. Three seamen and a woman were quarrelling, trying to force their way into the building. When the police arrived there was a fight and Inspector Adams was stabbed below the heart. Two constables ran for their cutlasses and with the assistance of Henry Lovett, an ex-army officer and owner of the nearby "Windsor Hotel," tried to quell the affray. Lovett was also stabbed before the three sailors and woman were arrested. Both Adams and Lovett recovered from their wounds.

"The Ship Hotel" finally closed at about the same time as the docks began to decline. "The Dock Hotel" and "The Marine Hotel" closed at the same time.

One of the best-known pubs in the area was the "Penarth Railway Hotel" which, for many years, was referred to as "The Red House." Standing just outside the docks, on land reclaimed from Penarth Flats, it was regularly frequented by sailors from the ships using the tidal harbour. In 1847 the sailing vessel "Catherine" landed twenty-five illegal immigrants, Irishmen intent on making a new life for themselves, on the mud in front of "The Red House." The ship's captain was caught, fined twenty pounds and given two months in prison for the offence.

The most renowned landlord of "The Red House" was Captain Andrew Garrick. Many Victorian landlords had secondary occupations - Christopher Hill of "The Golden Lion" was a shipwright, Job David of "The Merrie Harrier" was a farmer. And Andrew Garrick was a Master Mariner.

In August 1908 Garrick's sailing ship "Amazon" was caught in one of the worst gales ever to hit the south Wales coast. Anchored to the east of Mumbles, the "Amazon's" port cable parted and she was driven onto Margam Sands at 8.00 am on 31st August. Her fore, main and mizzen masts were carried away and such was the severity of the wind and sea that none of the rescuers could get near. Twenty one of the crew, including Captain Garrick, were drowned in the disaster.

The wreck of the "Amazon" on Margam Beach in 1908. Captain Garrick, who was also the landlord of "The Red House" pub in Penarth, was drowned in the disaster along with most of his crew.

"The Red Lion" has only recently closed its doors for the last time. Redevelopment work in the immediate area has caused the closure but it is another sad loss, another sad break with the historic past of Penarth.

A number of drinking clubs existed in the town at the end of the nineteenth century. These were places where sailors and visitors could find a welcome and a drink at almost any time of the day or night. The clubs included establishments like "The Central Club" and "The Clive Club", the latter occupying the site of the present day "Railway Hotel." A renowned drinking den and a place to, apparently, find ladies of dubious virtue, was "The Clifton Club." It ran for some twenty years at the end of the century.

"The Windsor Hotel" was one of the original public houses in the town, being opened in 1856. The hotel actually had its own brewery for a while and was originally located at the corner of Windsor Road and Maughan Street. The 1871 census return gives the name of the licensee as Henry Lovett who ran the place with his son Frederick. The son was also the agent for the Iman Shipping Line, yet another example of pub owners and managers with more than one job.

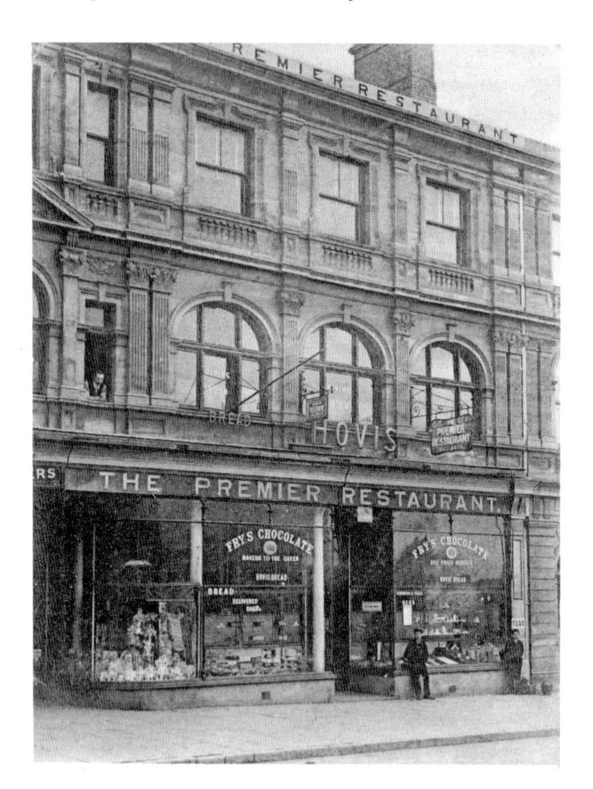

Visitors to Penarth were well catered for in public houses, cafes and restaurants. This view shows The Premier Restaurant next to the Windsor Arcade.

"The Windsor Hotel" was the scene of a famous murder in 1869 when a young woman from Cardiff smashed in the head of one Michael Toomy. Apparently she held a large stone in her fist and used it with startlingly effective results on the skull of the unsuspecting Toomy.

"The St Fagan's Castle" was another early pub in the town. It was certainly in existence by 1861 when the census return gives the name of the licensee as David Evans. The three horse breaks of Solomon Andrews used to leave for Cardiff from a spot directly opposite the pub. Obviously "The St Fagan's Castle" was the ideal place to sit and wait for the carriages to appear!

With the addition of tea rooms and cafes, both in the town and down on the Esplanade, visitors to Penarth were certainly well provided for. A complete infrastructure had grown up around the twin elements of industry and tourism. By the beginning of World War One the people of Penarth might be excused for sitting back and smiling, a little smugly, congratulating themselves on how well they had done.

A street scene in Penarth.

Chapter Four

Depression, War - and a Little Bit More

Penarth, as a holiday resort, had relied heavily on its pier from the time it was opened in 1895. When the pier was returned to the Company after war service, in 1919, the degree of damage to the structure shocked everyone. Most of the significant wear and tear was located on the landing stage - one of the main reasons the Pier Company had been unsuccessful in its claim for compensation. This jetty was made from greenheart timber and, like all wooden structures, needed constant and careful attention, the type of attention any Piermaster and his staff would give as a matter of course. During the war years the landing stage had received virtually no attention at all.

The Penarth Pier Pavilion Programme for 1922. The pier might be in dire need of restoration at this time but Alfred Newton, who ran the entertainments, was determined to make a go of things.

The AGM of the Pier Company was held on 4th December 1922 when John Cory, the Chairman, declared that repairing the landing stage was out of the question. The Company could not afford it and if any work were to be carried out then the Company would be looking to the Penarth public to subscribe the necessary money, either in shares or in debentures.

A dilapidated pier was largely unusable, apart from some limited degree of promenading. It was, if anything, a deterrent to trade in the town. Campbell's paddle steamers had renewed their excursions in the summer of 1919 but the landing stage was in such poor condition that they were unable to call at Penarth that year. Before the war around 35,000 trippers each season had used the pier to embark on the paddlers. With Penarth Pier now out of action most of those people went either to nearby Barry or to the Pier Head in Cardiff - with the resulting loss of trade for the town and people of Penarth.

During the 1923 season there was considerable debate in council chambers and in the press about the possibility of

Penarth Urban District Council taking over control of the pier. The Council was certainly very interested in the prospect but discussions dragged on and while the Councillors debated, Penarth, to use something of a mixed metaphor, was almost dying on its feet.

On August Bank Holiday that year over 70,000 people visited Barry Island. St Mary's Well Bay, Swanbridge and Sully - tiny resorts with almost no facilities - received 19,000 trippers. Penarth, without its pier, had less than 10,000. Local tradesmen gritted their teeth and dreamed of the day when the pier would finally be open again.

A Punch and Judy Show on the beach - traditional seaside entertainment.

In the summer of 1924 the deal was done at last and a purchase price of £5000 was paid by the Council to the Pier Company. The Pier Directors might, perhaps, be excused for rubbing their hands together in glee. Not only had they got rid of a huge albatross from around their necks, they had actually received a rather large sum of money into the bargain. The Council quickly realised that the damage to the pier was worse than had previously been thought and it was estimated that at least £20,000 would be needed to repair the landing stage. However, it would be money well spent if it brought the vital tourist trade back to the town. Up grading of the Esplanade had already begun, part of the Council's scheme of post-war improvements for the town, but work on the pier was delayed for some time. It was a complicated process and finding the right people for the job was important.

Work finally began in 1925 with the first ferro-concrete pile being driven into the sea bed at low water on the afternoon of 11th May. New decking was laid on the pier itself and on the landing stage while the landward end was widened to allow for the erection of a brand new pavilion. Designed to hold 600 people, this new pavilion was to be a modern, user-friendly facility that also housed shops, cloakrooms, a tea lounge and a terrace or promenade on each side of the building.

This wonderful photograph shows the new pavilion on the pier in the early stages of construction.

Up and Running Again

After numerous delays the landing stage opened for business again on Wednesday 7th April 1926. Between April and Whit Sunday a limited paddle steamer service was offered by P and A Campbell but after that it was a full programme of cruising for the first time since the summer of 1914.

Income from pier tolls had increased sharply since the Urban District Council took control at the end of 1924. Despite this there continued to be delay after delay over the completion of the new pavilion. The work dragged on and to the people of Penarth it seemed that it would never be finished. Finally, on 9th May 1929, the "Penarth Times" was able to gleefully announce -

"The New Pavilion, which Penarth has been waiting for so long, will be opened on Saturday evening next - - - The opening night promises to be one of the biggest social events ever held in Penarth."

With the new pavilion finished and open for business 1929 promised to be a good year for Penarth. The pavilion was certainly an imposing structure, dominating the more elegant Victorian buildings in the area.

After the low number of visitors in the 1920s, Penarth finally seemed to be back in the fight once the new pavilion opened. People flocked to the town to stroll and embark on the paddle steamers.

An advert for the "Modern Follies", the opening act of the 1930 season on Penarth Pier.

The new pavilion was a unique structure, being constructed entirely from ferro-concrete. It was a massive building, if not exactly beautiful then certainly impressive. Built by Messrs E J Smith of Cardiff, the pavilion sat on the landward end of the pier and dominated the immediate surroundings. It was not unlike a beached whale in appearance and gave local wags a great source of material for jokes and humorous anecdotes. Nevertheless, no matter what the sceptics might say, the pavilion was finished at last.

The official opening took place at 5.00pm on 18th May. There were speeches from Councillors and solos from Madame Venn and Miss Doris Pawley before proceedings were brought to a close with the singing of the Welsh National Anthem. The District Council and the whole town now looked to the future with hope, relief and enthusiasm.

By 1930 Penarth could boast two pavilions on its pier - and both of them were well used.

The Penarth Pier Fire.

THE BLAZING PIER.

THE SCENE NEXT MORNING.

Disaster!

On the evening of Monday 3rd August 1931 disaster struck when the old Bijou Pavilion and part of the pier itself were destroyed by fire. It has never been clear how the fire began although, in all probability, it was caused by a discarded cigarette end falling through the floorboards of the old pavilion and igniting the accumulated rubbish lying there beneath.

After smouldering away for some time the fire suddenly erupted at about 9.00pm. Soon the whole pier was ablaze and thirty people, trapped on the landing stage, had to be evacuated by boats from the Yacht Club. When dawn came the following day the pier was a mass of twisted metal and at first sight the damage seemed terminal. The only positive side to the disaster came when children of the town found dozens of coppers on the beach below the pier - they had fallen from the buckled and melted slot machines.

The appearance of the pier was deceptive, however. Council engineers quickly discovered that the damage was not as serious as previously thought and the main structure seemed relatively sound. It was, surprisingly, still usable for the paddle steamers and so the Council simply erected a gangway over the burned sections of the walkway and turned their thoughts to reconstruction.

The pier was rebuilt within a year, at a total cost of £3157 but the Bijou Pavilion, much to the regret of many Penarth people, was not replaced. The new building, so recently opened, would, it was felt, be sufficient to cater for the needs of holiday makers.

A Time of Change

The 1930s were a time of great change, a time of almost universal Depression and unemployment. In Wales, where much of the economy was based around the coal, iron and steel industries of the southern valleys, there was considerable hardship. Unemployment was rife. As far as Penarth was concerned people no longer came to spend weeks in the seaside town, promenading on the pier and strolling along the Esplanade. They had neither the money nor the inclination.

Some visitors did come, albeit mainly for day trips. It was small consolation and several local traders went out of business at that time. In 1932, in an effort to keep its head above water, the pier pavilion was turned into a cinema. As a business enterprise the project failed and was closed the following year. The pavilion was redesigned as a dance hall and, as the Marina Ballroom, opened its doors in October 1934. Later known as the Commodore, the dance hall was a popular location for people in the Cardiff and Penarth area for many years. Sadly, these days it has neglected and empty look, perhaps more like a beached whale than ever.

Over the years a number of cinemas had existed in Penarth. From the early days of the moving image the people of Penarth had flocked to these cinemas to watch the antics of Charlie Chaplin, Buster Keaton and the rest. According to Alan Thorne in "Place Names of Penarth" the first cinema in the town was the Cinema Theatre, operating out of a converted shop in Glebe Street. That was in 1910. Other well-known Penarth cinemas included the Empire Palace, the Gem and the Windsor.

The best remembered cinema in the town, however, is the Washington which opened for business in April 1938. It was run by the Willmore brothers, the same family that had owned the Cinema Theatre in earlier times, and operated in the centre of town for many years.

The Windsor Cinema opened in 1914 and remained operational for over forty years. It was run by Miss Maude Jefferies, one of the few women cinema managers in Britain. The Windsor closed its doors for the last time in 1958 but the building can still be seen close to Dingle Road railway station.

Penarth acquired its own Maternity and Child Welfare Centre in 1925. Known as the Catherine Jenkins Institute, the centre was located in a house in Stanwell Road and played a useful role in offering meals and care to children whose families had been hit by the Depression.

Penarth Dock, seen here from the air in the 1930s, almost at the end of its life.

Penarth Docks suffered particularly badly during the Depression years. The total trade in the docks dropped from just over a million and a half tons a year in 1931 to below 700,000 in 1936. Lay offs were common and the queues of unemployed men - a sight rarely seen in Penarth until then - stretched like a long winding sheet around the streets of the town. It was only the coming of war in 1939 that really brought any degree of prosperity back to the community.

War Once More

When war was declared in September 1939 its effect on Penarth was immediate. Within a few days Campbell's had suspended their paddle steamer service in the Bristol Channel in the face of possible U Boat attacks. Several of their paddlers were quickly called up for war duty, three of them - "Devonia," "Brighton Queen" and "Brighton Belle" - being sunk at Dunkirk. The fondly remembered "Waverley" was also lost later in the war.

Almost immediately Penarth Pier was closed to the public although some restricted use returned as the war went on. Pier personnel like Piermaster J A Kinnersley RNR either enlisted in the services or were called up for duty.

A large number of young men and women from Penarth enlisted in the forces and, sadly, many died on active service. The docks had reopened shortly after war began and, as a consequence, the town suffered a number of air raids between the summer of 1940 and the following autumn. In total, seven Penarth residents lost their lives in these raids, many more being seriously injured.

At the beginning of the war two six-inch guns were mounted on the cliff above the Esplanade. Manned by troops of the Glamorgan Heavy Artillery, these guns were the descendants of the weapons place there during World War One but they did not last long in Penarth. Early on in the war, the weapons were removed and a battery of modern, more effective three-inch artillery pieces located in Cardiff Docks.

The old searchlight platforms at the bottom of Penarth Head provided "an illuminated area" in case of attack by surface craft or submarines. Searchlights and guns out on Flat Holm Island, like the bases in Cardiff and Penarth, came under the control of 570 Coast Regiment.

As the war progressed restrictions on the use of Penarth Pier were gradually relaxed. As early as January 1941 old age pensioners were given permission to fish off the pier again while, in May 1943, the Council ordered that deckchairs could once more be placed on the decking during daylight hours. Previously they had been considered too much of a fire risk should the pier be bombed. The relaxation of such restrictions may have been slight but they were a sure sign that victory would be bound to arrive soon.

Peace Returns

When the German army surrendered on Luneburg Heath in April 1945 the Council and the leaders of Penarth turned their minds, once more, to the mundane business of making a living. The main need in these immediate post-war years was to provide adequate housing for the people of the town.

In 1946 fifty "prefab" houses were erected on Redlands Avenue. Simple to build and cheap to maintain, prefabricated houses became a common feature in most Welsh towns over the next few years. New estates were created in several parts of Penarth and in July 1952 the Council's 500th post-war house was opened in St David's Crescent. By 1963 over one thousand new council houses and 730 private dwellings had been built in the eighteen-year period since the end of the war.

Penarth Dock closed again once war ended. And this time the closure was permanent. Two old German sailing ships, the "Pamir" and "Passatt," were moored in the dock for a brief period at the end of the 1940s. Due to be scrapped, the two vessels were eventually converted into training ships but when the "Pamir" was lost at sea in 1957 the idea of training seamen on board old fashioned sailing ships went down with her.

Campbell's steamers renewed their Bristol Channel service in 1946, initially with just three paddlers. Penarth Pier, unlike many of the long, deep water piers of the Channel, was available for immediate use and when Campbell's launched two brand new paddle steamers , "The Bristol Queen" and "The Cardiff Queen," it seemed that the future of Penarth as a holiday destination was firmly secured.

Shipwreck!

On the evening of Friday 2nd May 1947 the Canadian steamer "Port Royal Park" collided with the pier. The ship was en route from Newport to Cardiff Docks where she was due to take on cargo and depart for the Persian Gulf. At 7131 tons she was a large vessel and, with a strong gale blowing, the tides of the Bristol Channel took her beyond the entrance to Cardiff Dock. Before Captain, Pilot or crew realised what was happening the ship was driven dramatically into the north side of Penarth Pier.

A dance was being held in the Marina Ballroom at the time and the revellers were blissfully unaware of their danger until the crash and vibration brought reality home, literally with a bang. The ship's bows finished up only a few feet away from the ballroom. Disaster was averted when Mr J A Brown, superintendent of Penarth Baths, saw a gas pipe on the pier fracture under the impact. Racing across the road, he cut off the gas supply and prevented a major explosion.

A second disaster took place in 1947 when the "Port Royal Park" hit the pier in a gale. Serious damage was sustained to the pier, as this photograph shows.

The "Port Royal Park" lay broadside on to the pier, her giant superstructure dwarfing the buckled planking. News of the accident spread quickly through the town and soon, despite the weather, thousands of spectators were lining the Esplanade for a view of the marooned vessel. The "Port Royal Park" was pulled off by tugs the following morning and towed into Cardiff for repair.

The "Port Royal Park" lying against the north side of the pier, before tugs came to drag her away.

It was obvious that the pier had suffered serious damage. The decking was buckled and shattered, almost for its entire length, while the northern shelter had been smashed into the centre of the walkway. Over 70 of the cast-iron supporting columns and pillars had been fractured.

Despite serious reservations about the extent of the damage, repair work began almost immediately. It took over eighteen months to complete and cost in the region of £28,000. The official re-opening took place on Whit Sunday 1949, to the great relief of the businessmen of Penarth and the devotees of the White Funnel Fleet.

Campbell's Steamers - the End of an Era

In the early 1960s Campbell's were still operating six paddlers and one turbine steamer in the Bristol Channel. Yet they were finding it increasingly difficult to make ends meet as the gradual availability of private motor cars ate into their trade and public tastes began to change. By the middle years of the '60s the company had "rationalised" itself to such an extent that the two "Queen's" were the only paddle steamers left in service.

Miners Fortnight, the two-week break at the end of July and beginning of August, had become traditional for industrial workers after the end of the war. It brought some degree of relief, both to Campbell's and to Penarth. By 1958 the town could still boast two hotels, four large guest houses and over 70 boarding houses. Sadly, the mini-boom was not to last.

During the summer of 1963 a unique Hovercraft Service had been operated by the White Funnel Fleet, running from Penarth beach to Weston-super-Mare. It was an unusual service at the time and did not last long - almost a desperate last throw of the dice, many people felt, by Campbell's. The gamble, like the paddle steamers, was doomed to failure.

Another crisis occurred when the "Bristol Queen" became the second vessel to hit Penarth Pier. The accident took place on 20th August 1966 when the paddler smashed into the woodwork in a thick fog. As the "Bristol Queen" had hit the walkway, not the landing stage, the steamer trips were not greatly affected.

The "Bristol Queen" and "Cardiff Queen" were withdrawn from service in the 1960s, leaving only motor vessels like "St Trillo" and "Balmoral" to fly the Campbell company flag. Penarth Pier had suffered and declined in importance along with the paddle steamers as foreign holiday destinations began to lure people away from the Bristol Channel. It was an impossible battle and finally, in 1980, the White Funnel Fleet went out of business, the end of over a hundred years of cruising on the waterway.

Under the terms of the Local Government Act of 1972 Penarth became part of the newly created South Glamorgan County. It was an important decision as Penarth had always been conscious of its status as a town apart and separate from the nearby city of Cardiff. Indeed, on a number of occasions Cardiff had attempted to incorporate Penarth, something that had always been resisted with great vigour by the smaller community. Ribbon development may now join Penarth with Wales' capital city but, apart from that, the two communities remain resolutely apart - as they have always been.

The Pier in all its glory, complete with paddler off on a trip down Channel to Lundy or Ilfracumbe or perhaps Weston. Notice the large number of sailing vessels moored off the Pier - a busy summer scene in the early years of the 20th century.

Chapter Five

People, Places and a Few Events

People make a town and Penarth, like any small, tightly knit community, has always had its fair share of famous characters. It would take a book on its own to even begin to do justice to the many people who have contributed to the growth of the place - the following few pages give a brief account of just some of the individuals who have helped make Penarth what it is today.

Windsor Gardens, created above the sea front in 1880. Notice the bridge that connected the two parts of the garden.

The Windsor-Clive Family

From the earliest days the Windsor-Clive family, the Earls of Plymouth, had always been great benefactors to Penarth. It was the marriage in 1730 of the quaintly named Other Archer, 6th Earl of Plymouth, to Elizabeth, the daughter of Thomas Lewis of St Fagan's, that brought the land and manor of Penarth under the control of the Plymouth family.

When the Earl died without children in1833 the family line was continued by his sister Harriet. She had married the Hon Robert Henry Clive, grandson of the famous Clive of India, in 1819 and the family name was changed to Windsor-Clive. They are names that, these days, linger on in the streets and buildings of Penarth. So, too, do names from Clive's famous Indian years - Arcot and Plassey being the best known.

When Robert Henry Clive died in 1854 Lady Harriet managed to terminate the abeyance of the Barony. She duly became Baroness Windsor and over the next dozen or so years patronised the new town that she had, largely, been instrumental in creating. Her son, Robert Clive, continued the benevolence and it was due to his enthusiasm - whatever the motivation - that most of the work on the Esplanade was finally completed.

Giving money and land to the developing town was just one part of the Plymouth family benevolence. Attendance at events in Penarth, by one or more family members, became common. And there were several recorded instances of patronage towards Penarth tradesmen. In 1889, for example, Penarth architect Henry Snell was commissioned to draw up plans for improving St Fagan's Castle - a clear case of "keeping it in the family."

Inspector Stephen Adams

Penarth Police Station was built in 1864 and placed under the control of newly promoted Inspector Stephen Adams. He was 43 years old at the time, having come from his native village of Llandysilio in Pembrokeshire to pursue his career in the police force. He had previously served in places such as Llantwit Major and Cowbridge before being appointed Sergeant at Llandough Police Station.

Adams viewed his new job at Penarth with enthusiasm. There was certainly much to do. Penarth, during the early part of his tenure as Inspector, was a wild, dangerous place to live. The drunken activities of sailors and dock workers kept the policemen very busy - there were, after all, just four of them at this time. The affray where Adams was stabbed in 1869 (see earlier) was just one instance or example of a policeman's duties.

Adams certainly served Penarth well. With his three constables (PCs Karn, Williams and Thomas) he was instrumental in making the streets of the town a much safer place for ordinary citizens.

John Batchelor

John Batchelor, the well-known "friend of freedom," is perhaps best remembered by his statue in the Hayes in Cardiff - invariably, when the University is in session, he wears a traffic cone on his head or outstretched arm. Most people, however, are unaware of his Penarth connections.

An early supporter of Chartism, Batchelor was a wealthy shipyard owner. He was Mayor of Cardiff in 1866 but, after living in several homes in the city, in 1867 he moved his family to the more healthy air of Penarth. He lived, first, at Cliff Villa on Penarth Head, overlooking the River Ely, but by the end of the decade had moved to Upper Cliffe House on the top of the headland. The house later became the Officers Mess of the

Garrison Artillery when a fort was built on the site.

Batchelor worked tirelessly for under-privileged people in Penarth and Cardiff and was the first Chairman of the Penarth School Board. He was one of the prime movers of the Ely Tidal Harbour and Penarth Dock scheme and actually suggested the building of a sea wall between Penarth Head and Cardiff Docks - a far-seeing man indeed.

The statue of John Batchelor, Friend of Freedom, in the Hayes, Cardiff.

Three Famous Visitors

On 11th May 1897 the Italian radio pioneer Marconi transmitted his historic first radio signal across water from Williams' Farm, Lavernock Point, to Flat Holm Island. Marconi had made his base at the farm for several weeks before the broadcast and was assisted by Cardiff Post Office engineer George Kemp. The first message to Flat Holm was sent in morse code, the dots and dashes being marked down on a tape. Only later were audio methods of communication introduced. And the contents of that ground breaking message? The simple phrase "Are you ready?"

Alfred Sisley, the French Impressionist painter, visited Wales for a three month period, also in 1897. During that time he spent a considerable period in Penarth and even painted a number of pictures set in the surrounding area. Perhaps the most famous of these is "Cliffs at Penarth," a view from the Cliff Walk, looking back towards the Esplanade and sea front. Another painting from the same period shows shipping in the Channel off Penarth and includes a distant view of the pier.

In July 1897 Sisley wrote to a friend that he had just arrived in Penarth, after a tiring journey from the south of England -

"The country is pretty and the shipping lane, with the great boats which go in and out of Cardiff, is superb."

On Wednesday 27th July 1921 His Royal Highness the Duke of York - later crowned King George V1 - came to Penarth to carry out the official opening of the J A Gibbs Home. After calling at the offices of the District Council and inspecting local scouts and cubs, the Duke went on to the newly established Gibbs Home. He duly inspected a Guard of Honour made up from cadets at the Home and watched a march past that included a field gun and dozens of eager trainees, all ready for "the essential calling of the sea."

The Duke of York came to Penarth in 1921 to officially open the J A Gibbs Home. This card shows him inspecting the Home's Guard of Honour. The naval officer behind the Duke is Lt Commander Carr, the nautical instructor at the Home. He was one of the few men on the staff as the place was run by women, the Methodist Sisters.

After a formal luncheon of seven courses and a programme of music provided by the band of the Glamorgan Garrison Artillery, the Duke of York visited the Mission to Seamen in the docks. This mission had been established in 1872, the aim being to provide light refreshments and a reading room for visiting seamen. After a quick visit to the Penarth Ex-Servicemen's Club - the Duke himself having served in the trenches during World War One - the royal visitor left for Cardiff station and home.

Dr Joseph Parry

Joseph Parry, arguably Wales' most famous composer, was born in poverty in Merthyr Tydfil in 1841. Despite his obvious musical talent, he began his working life in a coal mine, earning the princely sum of two shillings and sixpence each week. His parents emigrated to the USA when Joseph was twelve years old and, despite misgivings, the young musician went with them.

After working, initially, in an iron foundry Joseph's musical talent soon came to the fore and he returned to Britain to study at the Royal Academy. Professor of Music at Aberystwyth from 1874 until 1880, he moved south and became lecturer in music at Cardiff University.

Joseph Parry lived in Penarth for some years. Renowned as Wales most famous composer, he lectured at Cardiff University.

From 1888 Parry lived in Penarth, playing the organ each Sunday in Christchurch and revelling in the title of "the great Doctor." He settled in a house called "Cartref" in Victoria Road, a house he was later able to buy thanks to a donation of £630 from the Parry Testimonial Fund.

Joseph Parry was, to some extent, a man of unfulfilled talent and ambition. His best known works remain the hymn tunes "Aberystwyth" and "Myfanwy," long time essentials and sentimental favourites of all Welsh Male Voice Choirs. However, he did live to see his operas "Blodwen" and "Arianwen" become both popular and successful. He died in 1903 and is buried in the graveyard at St Augustine's Church. Apparently the funeral procession was so long that, as the hearse carrying his body was arriving at the church door, the last members of the procession were only just leaving his house, about a mile away.

The Rev. Elvet Lewis

The Rev Elvet Lewis lived in Penarth during the years of his retirement, often preaching at Christchurch. Born in 1860, he was a minister in London for many years but it is as a Welsh language poet that he is best remembered. He won the Bardic Crown at the National Eisteddfod in 1888 and the Chair six years later.

Between 1923 and 1927 Elvet Lewis was the Arch Druid of Wales. He died in 1954 but his name lives on in the Penarth area, Elved Avenue being named in his honour.

The town library was opened in 1905 alongside Christchurch in Stanwell Road. Christchurch has now gone but the library still operates from the same building. The entrance to the library was originally in Stanwell Road.

This view shows the lodge and entrance to Alexandra Park, named after the wife of King Edward VII. The donkeys in the photograph are presumably on their way to the nearby beach.

Penarth Places

While people are obviously important they have to operate within the confines of physical locations. Therefore, the places of Penarth - many of which have already been referred to or described - provide the context within which individuals lived and worked.

Alexandra Park, named after the wife of King Edward V11, was laid out on land above the sea front and donated to the town by the Windsor family. It was opened on Wednesday 25th June 1902 and boasted a fine shelter and bandstand. Concerts were held there on a regular basis, even as late as the 1930s.

The Dingle Bridge. Several "dingles" existed in Penarth, sleepy little areas that were ideal for a spot of courting.

There are several dingles around Penarth, the term being used to describe a wooded dell or valley. The classic example in Penarth is the one that runs through Windsor Gardens, leading the walker down the slope towards the Esplanade. It remains a quiet, secluded spot, much as it would have been during the early years of the twentieth century when it offered a peaceful haven for young lovers on their walk up from the sea front to the town's main railway station.

Windsor Gardens were laid out in 1880, as part of the "grand scheme" of Robert Forrest and Lord Windsor. A bridge crossed the path that led from Marine Parade to the beach, thus joining the two halves of the garden. To the right of the bridge, behind the Yacht Club, stood a renowned "puzzle gate" that allowed visitors to leave the gardens but not re-enter.

The Italian Gardens were built on the Esplanade in 1926. Their creation was part of the Council's plan to up-grade the sea front and make an attractive, interesting area for visitors to see.

Donkeys were a popular entertainment on Penarth beach for many years. Children loved them but there are several recorded instances of cruelty by donkey owners towards their animals.

The beach at Penarth has always been a draw for youngsters. While their parents could stroll along the Esplanade or sit in deck chairs to admire the view, the famous Penarth donkeys were an obvious attraction for Victorian and Edwardian children. So popular were the donkey rides that the stretch of beach between the Yacht Club and the pier was always known as Donkey Beach. For many years the donkeys plodded along the beach or, when the tide was in, along the road above.

Penarth was not all about the easy entertainment of pier, park or picture house, however. The foundation stone for the town library was laid on 10th September 1904. Local Councillor Samuel Thomas, once described as "Penarth's Lloyd George," negotiated a gift of £4000 from the Carnegie Trust and a plot of land was given to the town by Lord Windsor. The library opened in 1905, replacing the old Reading Room that had previously existed in Arcot Street.

A Few Famous Events

Penarth has seen more than a few interesting moments over the years, many of them connected with the sea and the docks.

Isambard Kingdom Brunel's "Great Britain", the world's first ocean going, iron, propeller driven ship, was one of many famous vessels to call at Penarth. Indeed, it was from Penarth Docks that she left on her last voyage, easing out through the lock gates on 6th February 1886. Rounding the Horn the "Great Britain" ran into a hurricane and was eventually abandoned at Port Stanley in the Falkland Islands where she lay, derelict and half sunk, for many years. The ship was eventually brought back to Bristol in 1970, huge crowds gathering on Penarth Head to watch her being towed up the Channel.

Robert Falcon Scott and his ship the "Terra Nova" sailed past Penarth in June 1910, bound for the South Pole. This view shows Scott's ship and the escorting paddler "Ravenswood."

Robert Falcon Scott and his ship "Terra Nova" sailed past Penarth on 15th June 1910, bound for Antarctica and a failed attempt to reach the South Pole. She was pulled out of Cardiff Docks by the tug "Falcon" and escorted by the paddle steamers "Ravenswood" and "Devonia." Thousands of day trippers and Penarth residents flocked to the sea front to watch Scott's departure.

Scott himself was not planning to stay on board the "Terra Nova" for long as he still had to raise money for the expedition. The party had already spent seven days in Cardiff, gathering funds and being wined and dined by the civic authorities. Cardiff actually became the largest single financial supporter of Scott's doomed enterprise. Scott left the "Terra Nova" almost as soon as the tug dropped her tow off Penarth Pier and set off to lecture at a series of fund raising events before rejoining the ship in New Zealand. Perhaps he would have been better off remaining on board and planning his attempt on the Pole - bad organisation that put pride and duty before strategy and tactics resulted in failure to reach the Pole before the Norwegian Amundsen. As all the world knows, Scott and four of his assault team died on the journey back from the South Pole.

On 3rd July 1932 the "Graf Zeppelin" cruised over Penarth and the surrounding area. This photograph was taken at the time by Mr C F Best and shows the zeppelin passing over Sully.

Visitors from the air arrived over Penarth in the summer of 1932. On 3rd July the German dirigible "Graf Zeppelin" flew across the town at a height of just over one thousand feet. People poured into the streets to witness the visitation, watching as the "Graf Zeppelin" cruised in a leisurely fashion over Penarth and Cardiff before turning southwards and disappearing from view.

One of the most interesting and unusual events in Penarth's history occurred on Friday 31st May 1901 when Educated Archie, the elephant from Sanger's Circus, collapsed and died in Stanwell Road. The elephant was parading from Newport to Penarth as the circus was shortly due to open in town. Archie lay, panting, on the ground for some time before finally dying. Apparently, Archie refused to eat anything while lying there but did manage to consume several bottles of whiskey and rum. It took six horses to pull the body into Solomon Andrews field.

After the end of World War One a tank from the Western Front was presented to the town. This was a common occurrence in Britain at the time and these huge old monstrosities stood for years in town squares, memorials to the fallen. The Penarth tank stood in Alexandra Park but it did not meet with everyone's approval. Many townspeople felt that it reminded them, and their children, of the carnage in the trenches. Whatever the debate, the Penarth tank remained in the Park until the early days of World War Two when, like many other pieces of iron and steel, it was towed away to be melted down and used in new weapons of war.

A hovercraft on Penarth beach in 1963. It was a short and ill-fated attempt to keep the White Funnel Fleet afloat but at least it gave visitors something to look at.

Francis Frith Collection

A number of shipwrecks took place around the Penarth area - as you would expect in a town intimately connected with the sea. Notable amongst them was that of submarine "L52" which, in 1935, was being towed to Llanelli for scrapping when she broke free from her tugs. She was adrift in the Bristol Channel for two days before being thrown up onto Sully beach.

The steamer "Pilton" was another vessel to end up on Sully beach. On passage to Barry, she was cast up onto the shingle on 27th December 1924. Sightseers flocked to the scene, many of them coming away with large amounts of coal from the ship's hold. The "Pilton" was eventually re-floated and towed into Barry for repair.

Above all, though, throughout the years Penarth has been a scene of quiet, easy going solemnity. It has always been a seaside resort but one without the hustle and bustle of places like Blackpool or Brighton - or even nearby Barry Island. A sedate walk along the Esplanade or an afternoon spent snoozing on the pier were, normally, the height of excitement for visitors. That was how the resort had been designed; that was how it was.

The SS "Pilton" went aground on Sully beach in 1924 - it took five months to re-float her.

Penarth Pier in the 1930s

Chapter Six

Industry and Sport

Penarth has always been a town closely connected with industry, firstly through the docks and then, in their wake, via the tourist trade. However, for a long time there were also several other industries of note located in and around the town.

There used to be an alabaster mine in Penarth, or to be precise in the place where Penarth was soon to be, but its exact location remains unclear. The alabaster was extracted from the cliffs or picked up on the foreshore and used for medicinal purposes by local people. It is also recorded that small coasters would regularly pull up on the beach to take on loads of alabaster but, more than that, nothing is known.

Being a coal exporting port, vessels sailing to Penarth Docks would usually arrive empty. They were, after all, coming to take on coal. When ships were empty (in ballast as it was known) they rode high in the water and were therefore at risk from squalls and all the vagaries of sudden weather changes. In order to counter this, most of them shipped huge stones in their holds, ballast stones as they were called, until they could dock and take on cargo.

When the coal went in, the ballast stones came out. Penarth had its own Ballast Wharf where these stones were landed and, often, dumped. Local builders were not unaware of the practice and many buildings in Penarth were actually built from these huge ballast stones. Lord Bute apparently employed a full time agent at his docks in Cardiff whose sole job was to sell such stones.

A private boatyard, owned by Charles Cooper, was opened on a stretch of beach below Penarth Head in 1863. After changing hands several times, by the outbreak of World War One the yards had four large building sheds and were producing, amongst other vessels, a number of pilot cutters for use in the Bristol Channel. The yards continued to build ships until after World War Two but all the remains have now vanished from sight beneath the Cardiff Bay Barrage work.

Over the years several quarries have existed in and around the town, some of them still operational in the early part of the twentieth century. Certainly there was a long and well-recorded tradition of quarrying in the town. Since Roman times there had been quarrying here and as late as the sixteenth century there are records of Penarth stone being shipped to Newport for use in building sea walls.

An aerial view of the South Wales Portland Cement and Lime Co. works. A major employer in Penarth, the works closed in 1969.

Penarth Cement Works

The South Wales Portland Cement and Lime Company ran an operation that was located at Lower Penarth, limestone being quarried from huge pits that have now been flooded and incorporated into the Cosmeston Lakes complex. The works also produced high quality Portland cement.

A small railway was used to carry the limestone into the works, crossing Lavernock Road at a time when road traffic was still minimal. There was a small halt or station at Lower Penarth, opened mainly for use by workers at the Cement factory, but once mechanisation began to change the process of making cement the workforce was drastically reduced and the halt closed. By the early 1960s the works was still employing over 200 men.

In 1969, however, the Cement Works finally closed. The two locomotives that had been operating within the works were taken to Whipsnade where they were subsequently used to transport visitors around the zoo. Closure of the works meant that Penarth was suddenly left with no major industry, apart from tourism, able to employ large numbers of people. It was a far cry from the heady days when the docks were in full swing and unemployment was unheard of in the town.

Penarth Fire Brigade

Penarth's first fire engine was in service by 1875, being housed in Britannia Buildings on the corner of Glebe and Plassey Streets. It was privately owned by an insurance company and, in the early days, was horse drawn. Within a few years the engine had been relocated and was garaged at the town's police station but the engine continued to be pulled by horses, the animals having to be brought from Solomon Andrews stables in Ludlow Lane - hardly the most convenient of systems. In 1905, however, a motorised fire engine was purchased, costing in the region of £1000 and holding 500 gallons of water.

A purpose-built fire station was finally created in Albert Road a few years later. It was located next door to the Council Offices and here the part-time crew would drill and work on the engine. The fire engine, steam powered and heated by paraffin, had been built by Merryweathers, a firm specialising in making fire appliances.

Penarth Fire Brigade on board their steam driven engine, c1911.

It was not until 1927 that a more up to date engine was obtained for the town. This new model had a ladder attached and was a state-of-the-art machine. The old 1905 Merryweather engine was duly sold to a farmer in Newport who apparently used it to pump water on his farm - hardly the most elegant of retirements but at least it was a useful way for the old machine to end its days.

For many years the Fire Brigade Chief was Captain Morris. He was probably the only full time fireman in the town but at least Penarth had a brigade. Before 1875 any fire in the town or docks had to make do with the services of the Cardiff engine. And that could take a long time to reach the source of the fire. Often the blaze was already out by the time the Cardiff appliance actually arrived.

Sport

Sport has always played an important or significant role in the life of Penarth. The idea of "work hard, play hard" quickly took hold in the community and it was not long before people from the town were achieving fame and success on both a national and international level.

Penarth Rugby Club was founded in 1879 and was soon a significant part of the Welsh rugby establishment. Richard Garrett was the club's first international, gaining his cap against the touring Maoris in 1888. He went on to gain further honours against all the Home Nations sides.

Other Penarth rugby internationals included G R Rowles, J M Dyke, Jack Bassett, M Rosser and Gomer Hughes.

Penarth Swimming Club was created in 1896, using the town baths as their base. Soon there was even a Water Polo Team operating out of the baths and Gus Taylor of the Penarth Swimming Club played for Wales. He went on to become a Water Polo referee at the Olympic Games on several occasions.

For a long while swimming out in the Bristol Channel, either from Flat Holm or Weston-super-Mare, was very popular. It was a dangerous business as the tides were always strong but in 1929 sixteen year old Edith Parnell successfully made the crossing from Weston to Penarth. She might have been the youngest to achieve the feat but the very first person to swim across the Bristol Channel was Kathleen Thomas from Penarth. Her 1927 crossing took over seven hours of hard, dogged effort.

Numerous small or local sports teams were established in the town, many of them being closely connected with the various churches and chapels. Rugby, soccer, cricket and hockey were all played on a regular basis. It was not long before Penarth could boast two tennis clubs and a highly successful bowling tem as well.

Above all there was table tennis and a number of highly successful sides existed in Penarth. The YMCA and Tabernacle Chapel both had successful sides for many years but in 1932, after a split with the Tabernacle team, Park Table Tennis Club was formed. The name Park came into somebody's head as the "break away contingent" were walking towards the sea front through Alexandra Park one Sunday night.

Left to right, Glenys Thomas, Bob Bishop, Kim Johnson, Tony Johnson & Fraser Anderson of the Park Table Tennis Club at the Championships in Cardiff, early 1980s.

Kim Johnson in action.

The Park Club has produced a number of fine international players since 1932, people like Sid and Nan Matthews, Fred Grassoff and Kim Johnson while long serving player Tony Johnson became a renowned International Referee, officiating in events as far away as Korea and Yugoslavia. In the 1950s Jean Beer from the Park Club was the only woman to be capped by Wales using both the Penhold (Chinese) and, later, the English grip.

For the "upper echelons" of Penarth society there was always the game of golf. The Glamorganshire Golf Club on Lavernock Road is now recognised as one of the oldest clubs in Wales - not exactly the oldest as that honour goes to Tenby - but certainly one of the longest established. Glamorganshire was one of just seven clubs present at the inaugural meeting of the Welsh Golfing Union on 11th January 1895, the club being represented by Mr Herbert Flint.

The Glamorganshire club team won the 1905 Welsh Team Championship at Conwy, members of the victorious side including George Renwick who went on to win the Welsh Amateur title in 1906 and James Hunter, the Amateur Champion in 1902 and 1903. Also playing was the remarkable John Duncan who founded a Welsh golfing dynasty that has been unparalleled in the history of the game and whose name still lives on in the Duncan Putter competition for amateur golfers.

Glamorganshire Golf Club, one of the oldest clubs in Wales. This view shows the clubhouse and professional shop.

Above all Glamorganshire Golf Club is renowned as the place where the stableford system of scoring was invented. Dr Frank Stableford designed the eponymous scoring method whilst he was a member of the Penarth club, first trying out the system on members in 1898. The stableford system, a method that awards points according to a player's score on each hole, was based on the premise that one bad hole should not be allowed to spoil a whole round.

The first stableford competition took place at the Glamorganshire club on 10th September 1898 and was won by H Hastings Watson (42 points) who finished a full nine points ahead of the Rev. W E Shaw. Dr Stableford himself did not take part in the competition.

The Esplanade Hotel was the home of the Barbarians Rugby Club for many years - the club had been founded in the hotel in 1901.

Rugby, however, was always the first love of Penarthians. The famous Barbarians Rugby Football Club was founded in Penarth in 1901, the Esplanade Hotel on the sea front acting as their base until closure of the hotel in 1971 brought the connection to an end. The Barbarians game against Penarth had always been part of the club's traditional Easter tour to Wales but when the Esplanade closed and the Baa Baas moved their base to the Royal Hotel in Cardiff it signalled the end for the Penarth side. The last Penarth team to beat the Barbarians was actually the 1971 side but the fixture was dropped soon afterwards.

PENARTH			BARBARIANS	
15	Huw Powell		M. Rose *(Coventry & England)*	15
14	Robert Morgan		E. Rees *(Neath, Wales & British Lions)*	14
13	Damion Keen		N. J. Preston *(Richmond & England)*	13
12	Mike Gooding		J. Hewitt *(N.I.F.C. & Ireland)*	12
11	Mark Davies		C. Rees *(London Welsh, Wales, British Lions)*	11
10	Rod Crane		G. Pearce *(Bridgend & Wales)*	10
9	Alun Davies *(Capt.)*		I. J. Hunter *(Selkirk)*	9
1	Viv Crane	*Forwards*	G. S. Pierce *(Northampton & England)*	1
2	Mike O'Donnell		W. James *(Aberavon & Wales)*	2
3	Mike Davies		P. Rendall *(Wasps & England)*	3
4	Henry Bohlen		S. J. Perkins *(Pontypool & Wales)*	4
5	Martin Lewis		S. Bainbridge *(Gosforth & England)*	5
6	Chris Morgan		D. Richards *(Leicester)*	6
8	Robert Mc Pherson		G. Williams *(Bridgend & Wales)*	8
7	Julian Phillips		R. Best *(Harlequins)*	7

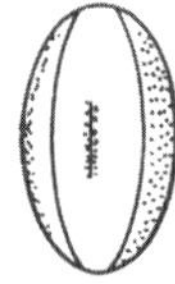

Replacements:
Curtis Taylor, David Rule

Referee:
K. C. Parfitt

REST OF TOURING PARTY

N. C. Stringer *(Wasps & England)*
M. Baily *(Cambridge University)*
J. Carlton *(Orrell, England & British Lions)*
J. Pollock *(Gosforth & Scotland)*
R. Ackerman *(London Welsh & Wales)*
D. Gerber *(South Africa)*
E. Tobias *(South Africa)*
M. Douglas *(Llanelli)*
N. Rowan *(Boroughmuir & Scotland)*
I. Stevens *(Bridgend, Wales & British Lions)*
K. Townley *(Llanelli)*
J. Condom *(Boucau & France)*
Clive Davis *(Newbridge)*
D. Cooke *(Harlequins & England)*
J'L Joinel *(Brieve & France)*
J. F. Imbernon *(Peppignan & France)*
P. Winterbottom *(Headingly & England)*

The Barbarians team full of internationals picked to play Penarth during their annual Easter visit to South Wales in 1983.

Scouts, Guides and Youth Organisations

The first scout patrol in Penarth was formed in 1908. Named the Ram Patrol, Hugh Pearce was Scout Master and S A Jones the Patrol Leader. The organisation grew quickly and soon there were two patrols. These were duly formed into the 1st Penarth Troop.

The Penarth scouts were inspected by the Duke of York when he came to open the Gibbs Home in 1921, the start of an interesting collaboration with the Gibbs Home as the branch soon had its own troop. Originally known as the J A Gibbs Home Troop, a later troop was called the 4th Penarth and also encompassed a cub pack. Scouting at the Home continued until after World War Two.

Girl Guides came to Penarth a little later. The 3rd Penarth All Saints Church Guide Company was formed in 1924, giving girls of the town the same opportunities for adventure and education as their male counterparts. The 6th Penarth Guides, based at Trinity Church, came into existence a few years later in January 1927.

The concept of Youth Clubs, as we know them today, is a fairly modern idea but the churches and chapels of Penarth all had youth groups from early on in their existence - sports clubs, Band of Hope, discussion groups and so on. As late as the 1960s and '70s the 2000 Club at Albert Road Church was a renowned and highly efficient Youth Club. Staffed by volunteers from the church and operating at the height of the new "drugs" craze, it did sterling work in the community and ran until the early '90s. The Boys and Girls Brigades both flourished in the town, being attached to the Methodist Church. They were regularly to be seen parading on Sundays and at important town events.

The Boys Brigade, one of the many youth organisations that operated in Penarth over the years.

Lifeboats and Coastguards.

Being both a maritime and tourist centre there was always a need for lifeboats in Penarth. The original Lifeboat House in the town was situated on the sea front, close to the area where the Yacht Club now stands. The town's first lifeboat was the "George Gay," quickly re-christened by Baroness Windsor on the opening day of Penarth Docks in1865.

A succession of lifeboats replaced the original one but in December 1881 the much larger "Joseph Denman 11" (a 12 oared, self righting pulling vessel) arrived on the scene. Too large for the Lifeboat House, she was kept moored at the entrance to the docks while a new Lifeboat House was built below Penarth Head.

Penarth lifeboat was only rarely called into service, however, as most of the distress calls went to other stations and in 1904 the place was closed. All that now remains is the inshore rescue boat, the present Lifeboat Station lying close to its original position alongside the Yacht Club.

The first Coastguard buildings in the area were built in the 1840s, before the town even existed, on the hill overlooking the Ely River and Penarth Flats. The coastguard boat was kept in a shed beneath the cliff. A second set of Coastguard Cottages was built in 1864, overlooking the beach and Esplanade on the other side of town. Alan Thorne, in "Place Names of Penarth," reckons that

"The Coastguard, which was an arm of the Royal Navy during the 19th Century, was inspected annually. In 1892 the inspector was Captain Bosanquet and in 1893 Prince Louis Battenberg, father of the late Lord Mountbatten did the honours."

Wreck and rescue in the Channel off Penarth were a constant problem. In June 1958, for example, the tug "Lavernock" collided with the "SS Hurunui," an 11,000 ton cargo ship, off Penarth beach. Only two years later the oil tanker "Regent Royal" ran aground on Penarth Head. And these accidents occurred long after the great days of Penarth Docks.

In the great freeze of 1963 there was a hazard of a different type when the sea at Penarth actually turned to ice. Small floes were seen on Penarth beach, lying grouped around the pier - a far cry indeed from the hot summers people normally associated with the town.

Chapter Seven

Up to Date

With the demise of Campbell's White Funnel Fleet the future of Penarth as a holiday destination seemed more than a little doubtful. Foreign destinations were increasingly claiming the holiday traffic - if people were content to spend their vacations in Wales then they either headed further west, to the Gower or Pembrokeshire coasts, or took a caravan at places like Trecco Bay in Porthcawl. Penarth's hotels and guest houses went into permanent decline.

Salvation came, however, with the advent of the day-tripper. As the 1970s and '80s unfolded Penarth began, increasingly, to offer itself as a day trip resort, a place people could drive to and enjoy for a few hours before returning to the comforts of their own homes. Central to that success was Penarth Pier.

Local Government re-organisation in 1974 had meant that the pier under-went another change of ownership. Since 1924 it had belonged to the Penarth Urban District Council. Now it came under the control of the new Vale of Glamorgan District of South Glamorgan County. Interestingly, the Town Council had hoped to retain control of the popular swimming baths - they were not too bothered about the pier. As it happened they lost both and the baths were eventually closed down after Cogan Leisure Centre was built.

A third, little known collision involving the pier took place in May 1984 when the 35 foot ketch "Thelme" was swept into the decking after her engine failed. Piermaster Thomas Fearnley lowered a rope ladder and the crew were able to scramble to safety. The owners of the yacht were still on board, however, and were rescued by the Penarth Inshore Lifeboat. A tug was called but the "Thelme" sank before the towline could be secured. For several days the wrecked yacht was a draw for visitors who were able to walk around the vessel at low tide. The pier was not damaged apart from some minor problems caused by the mast of the yacht to the roof of the toilet block.

Tom Fearnley was the last Piermaster at Penarth. He had succeeded Stan Galley in 1970, both men being famous names around the town. "The Western Mail" commented on Tom Fearnley's retirement in May 1985 that

"A quarter of a century ago the Piermaster was not just the Piermaster but he was a one-man tourist information centre. He would spend his day attending to the arrival of passenger boats at the end of the pier. There would be six or seven people employed on the pier to look after the boat, the deck chairs and the pier office."

Now, however, the Vale Council had decided that the services of a Piermaster were no longer required and Tom Fearnley was not replaced. Another important change came about at the same time when tolls for admission were also abolished. The pier was no longer to provide income but, rather, had become an amenity, paid for out of the rates. The old Directors of the original Pier Company were probably turning in their graves. After all, the pier had begun life as a private enterprise, something to make money. Now, it seemed, money was the last thing people expected the pier to make.

Paddle Steamers - Again

The Paddle Steamer Preservation Society had been founded in 1959 by a group of paddle steamer enthusiasts. "The Bristol Queen" and "The Cardiff Queen" had undoubtedly been scrapped a little prematurely but in 1974 the Society obtained the old Clyde steamer "Waverley." The re-vamped paddler now visits the Bristol Channel every year, her visits being increased in length as the renewed popularity of cruising grows and grows.

The "Waverley" off Penarth - cruising has come back to the Channel and to the town over the past few years.

In 1986 the "Waverley" was supplemented by the "Balmoral" and Penarth Pier has become the central point for Bristol Channel cruises. Over 30,000 people now tramp across the pier each year, just to embark on the cruise ships. The wheel really has come full circle.

The "Balmoral" is seen here off Penarth Pier early in 1988 season - before she has had time to be properly painted for the summer cruises.

For a brief period in the 1990s the state of the pier caused some anxiety. It was undoubtedly showing significant signs of wear and tear and rumours began to circulate that the Council was considering pulling it down. As a Grade 11 listed building and a major tourist attraction in south Wales there was an outcry when the word "demolition" was even thought about. Removal of Penarth Pier was not on the agenda, however, and repairs were carried out in time for the pier to celebrate its centenary in 1994.

New Marina

The once vibrant Penarth Docks had been a substantial affair, covering a huge amount of ground alongside the Ely River. After closure of the docks the old jetties were allowed to lie, dormant and rotting, for some time before the all powerful hands of developers reached out to take the area in their icy grasp. The inner part of the dock was filled in and, during the 1980s and '90s, housing, restaurants and a supermarket were built on the site.

The outer portion of the dock and basin were retained, however, and these were converted into an up-market marina, surrounded by modern housing. While the developments have caused wholesale destruction and devastation to Penarth's historic past, it is still good to see the area in use once again.

The Cardiff Bay Barrage, built and opened in the early years of the 21st century, has largely put an end to the banks of mud that were once such a feature of the bay.

The new marina at Penarth may have destroyed the last remains of the old dock but it has brought activity and a degree of prosperity back to the area.

The Ely River is no longer tidal and huge expanses of mud like Penarth Flats, once home to thousands of wading birds and other marine life, have sunk forever beneath the water. The area may now look a lot prettier, at least to the casual visitor, but much of the romance that surrounded the Flats has gone.

The last sad remains of Penarth Dock. Now even the mud has gone thanks to the Cardiff Bay Barrage.

It is strange to think that the vision of John Batchelor, the Penarth man who first suggested a barrage across the bay from Penarth to Cardiff, should have become reality at last. Putting aside all the debate, the points for and against such a barrage, it is interesting to imagine what Batchelor would think if he should suddenly come back to life. Hopefully, he would be pleased and try to see the positive points of the scheme.

The pier dominates the town in this modern aerial shot of Penarth. Cardiff might be close but it is a different community.

The Town.

The town of Penarth continues, in many ways much as it always did. Faced by competition from Cardiff and, increasingly, from out-of-town shopping complexes, many small businesses have found it difficult to survive. Others have changed their focus and have battled on, offering a vital service to the people of Penarth and its visitors. They remain an important part of the community.

Under re-organisation at the end of the 20th century the town came under the auspices of the newly created Vale of Glamorgan Council. For most of the people in Penarth there was a sense of relief - they would not be joined to the city and council of Cardiff. Independence was assured.

Penarth is a town with a wonderful past, one that is vibrant with enterprise and adventure. Its history is magnificent. Now it looks to the future with pride and hope.

Phil Carradice is an author and broadcaster who was written over 20 books. He is a novelist, poet and historian who regularly broadcasts on BBC radio and takes creative writing sessions for adults and children. He lived in Penarth for 15 years, being Headteacher of Headlands School, and now lives in the Vale of Glamorgan.

Bibliography.

Anon "South Wales Ports" pub by British Transport Commission. 1947

E Alwyn Benjamin "Penarth 1841 - 71" pub by D Brown and Sons. 1980

Peter Bennett and David Jenkins "Welsh Ports of the Great Western Railway" pub by the National Museum of Wales. 1994

Phil Carradice "Penarth Pier" pub by Quotes. 1994

Phil Carradice "Headlands School in Camera" pub by Barracuda Books. 1990

David Ings "Penarth in Old Picture Postcards" Vol 1 and 2 pub by the European Library. 1990

Alan Thorne "Place names of Penarth" pub D Brown and Sons. 1997

Roy Thorne "History of Penarth" pub by Starling Press. 1975

Eurwyn Williams "St Fagans Castle and its Inhabitants" pub by the National Museum of Wales. 1998

Stuart Williams "Glamorgan History, Vol One" pub D Brown and Sons. 1963

Acknowledgements.

Many thanks to the following for their help in sourcing and for permission to use various photographs.

Scanair UK
Judges Postcards Ltd
Windsor Bookshop Archive
Francis Frith Collection
Steve Ashby
D. K. Jones Collection
S. Rickard Collection
Tony Johnson
George Best
Phil Carradice
Andrew Quick
Brian Stephens
Percy Stephens

Every effort has been made to contact all copyright holders but this has not always been possible. If any readers can assist us in this area we will note acknowledgements in any further edition.